EVERY
CHRISTIAN
SHOULD KNOW

52

WORDS

Ken Easley
16 July 2006

HOLINESS

SOVEREIGNTY

OMNISCIENCE

EVERY
CHRISTIAN
SHOULD KNOW

52 WORDS

PRESENCE

LOVE

TRINITY

SCRIPTURE

INSPIRATION

INFALLIBILITY

THE LAW

PROPHECY

INTERPRETATION

KENDELL EASLEY

GREAT COMMANDMENTS

CREATION

IMAGE OF GOD

HOLMAN
REFERENCE

Nashville, Tennessee

52 Words Every Christian Should Know
Copyright © 2006 by Kendell H. Easley

ISBN 13: 978-0-8054-4058-4
ISBN 10: 0-8054-4058-5

B&H Publishing Group
Nashville, Tennessee
www.broadmanholman.com

Unless otherwise noted, all Scripture quotations have been taken from the *Holman Christian Standard Bible*® Copyright © 1999, 2000, 2002, 2003 by Holman Bible Publishers.

Dewey Decimal Classification: 230

Subject Heading: Christianity—Dictionaries\Devotional Literature\ Bible—Study

Printed in the United States of America
1 2 3 4 5 08 07 06

V

Dedicated to the glory of God
and in grateful appreciation
to my home congregation,
Germantown Baptist Church,
Germantown, Tennessee,
especially the
Perkins Friday Breakfast Fellowship

Contents

Introduction

Postmodern assumptions now dominate the North American conversation landscape, such as, "A term can mean whatever you want it to mean, for example, *marriage.*" Further, many who have been in church for years have only the fuzziest notions about the meaning of central biblical or theological terms. This implies an ever greater challenge for those engaged in Christian teaching and preaching. There is a place for a book for everyday believers that says, "Christian terms have standard meanings, and here are the historic, orthodox meanings of essential terms." The book in your hands was prepared for this reason.

Each of the 52 terms is presented in a two-page study, organized into 8 major biblical categories. All begin with a pertinent citation from the Holman Christian Standard Bible, continue with a concise definition, move on to a brief discussion, and close with thought questions and a devotional prayer. Why 52 terms? To learn about one Christian term each week for a year is a reasonable goal for even the busiest of persons.

I have written from a broadly evangelical perspective. My treatment is sensitive to areas where there are major differences of opinion, such as dispensational eschatology, Calvinism, Pentecostal issues, and the sacraments or ordinances. On the other hand, I affirm as a foundation the classic confessions of the churches (the Apostles' Creed and the Nicene Creed) and the five pillars of the Reformation (salvation as taught in Scripture alone, by Christ alone, by grace alone, through faith alone, to the glory of God alone). If you relate positively to these beliefs and want to gain a better understanding of essential Christian terms, this book is for you.

THE APOSTLES' CREED
(traditional wording; historically associated with baptism)

I believe in God, the Father Almighty, Maker of heaven and earth;
And in Jesus Christ His only Son our Lord,
Who was conceived by the Holy Ghost, born of the Virgin Mary,
Suffered under Pontius Pilate, was crucified, dead and buried;
(He descended into hell;)
The third day He rose again from the dead; He ascended into heaven,
And sitteth on the right hand of God the Father Almighty;
From thence He shall come to judge the quick and the dead.
I believe in the Holy Ghost; the holy catholic Church;
The communion of saints; the forgiveness of sins;
The resurrection of the body; and the life everlasting. Amen.

THE NICENE CREED

(traditional wording; historically associated with the Lord's Supper)

I believe in one God,
The Father Almighty, Maker of heaven and earth,
And of all things visible and invisible;
And in one Lord Jesus Christ,
The only-begotten Son of God,
Begotten of His Father before all worlds,
God of God, Light of Light, very God of very God,
Begotten, not made, being of one substance with the Father;
By whom all things were made;
Who for us men and for our salvation came down from heaven,
And was made incarnate by the Holy Ghost of the Virgin Mary,
And was made man;
And was crucified also for us under Pontius Pilate;
He suffered and was buried;
And the third day He rose again according to the Scriptures,
And ascended into heaven,
And sitteth on the right hand of the Father;
And He shall come again, with glory,
To judge both the quick and the dead;
Whose kingdom shall have no end.
And I believe in the Holy Ghost the Lord, and Giver of Life,
Who proceedeth from the Father and the Son;
Who with the Father and the Son together is worshiped and glorified;
Who spake by the Prophets.
And I believe in one holy catholic and apostolic Church;
I acknowledge one baptism for the remission of sins;
And I look for the resurrection of the dead
And the life of the world to come. Amen.

I. GOD

Who is God? What is He like? Thinking about these questions has driven the greatest thinkers and philosophers of the ages. In today's world, the issue—on the popular level at least—seems to be propelled by two notions. On one side is the idea that God is whatever or whoever the individual makes Him (or It or Her) out to be. Everybody's idea is equally valid. Do you want God to be like "the Force" of Star Wars? Fine, even though there's a dark side. Do you want God to be like a genie dispensing health and wealth for the asking? If this works for you, go for it. The other notion is driven by a growing awareness of the religion of Islam, which worships only one God. Many people have assumed that the God of Islam (Allah) and the God of Christianity must be identical. Thus the question arises, Is the God of Islam the Father of Jesus Christ? Are Muslims and Christians—both claiming to worship the only deity there is—serving the same God?

Christians begin with the Scriptures, not with popular culture or with someone's experiences of "God." Follow the study of these seven terms that point to the true identity of the God of the Bible. In particular, note the last study, on the Trinity. If, as orthodox Christians have always affirmed, God eternally exists in three Persons—Father, Son, and Spirit—then the answer to the two questions at the end of the previous paragraph must be a resounding no.

1. Glory

I saw the glory of the God of Israel coming from the east. His voice sounded like the roar of mighty waters, and the earth shone with His glory.... Then the Spirit lifted me up and brought me to the inner court, and the glory of the LORD filled the temple.   Ezekiel 43:2,5

DEFINITION: God's glory is the display of His greatness, goodness, and beauty so that persons are aware of Him through sensory experiences such as sight and sound. To glorify God means to respond to His revealed glory in the ways Scripture teaches, such as praise, love, joy, and obedience.

Glory in the Old Testament usually represents a word meaning heaviness or weight (Hebrew *kabod*). Not surprisingly therefore, human beings have often recognized God's glory in weighty or massive appearances: snow-capped mountains, starry skies, roaring oceans, or a splendid house of worship such as Solomon's temple or a medieval cathedral. God's majesty or worthiness was particularly revealed when His presence accompanied the Israelites from Egypt. When the cloud rested on Sinai, Moses saw God's glory (Ex 24:15-18). That glory was also associated with the tabernacle in the wilderness and the Jerusalem temple (Ex 40:34-35; 2 Ch 7:1-3). Many Jewish sources used the term *shekinah* (meaning "that which dwells," but not found in Hebrew Scripture) to refer especially to the manifested presence of God.

In the New Testament, the Greek word for glory is *doxa*, as in the title of the classic hymn, "The Doxology" (literally, "a word of glory"). In the Gospels God's glory was seen by shepherds at Jesus' birth and by the disciples throughout His ministry (Lk 2:9; Jn 1:14). Jesus' death and resurrection displayed the glory of God (Jn 12:23-28; Lk 24:26). The second coming of Jesus will powerfully reveal God's glory (Mk 8:38).

The Epistles teach that the glory of Christ and the glory of God are one and the same. The implications for followers of Christ are astounding. Paul told the Corinthians, "God, who said, 'Light shall shine out of darkness'—He has shone in our hearts to give the light of the knowledge of God's glory in the face of Jesus Christ" (2 Co 4:6). Thus, in the original creation, God's glory was manifested by the creation of light. Now in the new creation—sinners made into saints—God's glory has been experienced in human hearts, formerly dark places, "in the face of Jesus Christ."

Throughout the ages Christians have believed that God does all things for His glory. The logic is simply this: because God is the greatest, best, and most beautiful Being, then the most wonderful thing He can do is display Himself. This, in turn, means that human beings who have truly experienced His glory can't help but respond positively. To glorify God is to attach weight or worthiness to Him—and then to respond with all one's might (see Ps 150). One of the great documents of English speaking Christians, *The Westminster Confession,* famously stated, "The chief end of man is to glorify God and enjoy Him forever." Paul wrote, "Whether you eat or drink, or whatever you do, do everything for God's glory" (1 Co 10:31).

REFLECTION: Which displays of God's greatness, goodness, and beauty have moved you the most? How can you be more intentional about glorifying God day by day? Do you enjoy God? How?

PRAYER: Lord of glory, You have shown your greatness in all Your creation. You have revealed Your goodness through Jesus Christ. Your beauty is seen in all that You are and do. Teach us Your servants to glorify You through all our days unto eternity. Amen.

2. Holiness

Each of the four living creatures had six wings; they were covered with eyes around and inside. Day and night they never stop, saying: "Holy, holy, holy, Lord God, the Almighty, who was, who is, and who is coming."

Revelation 4:8

DEFINITION: Holiness is the quality of being set apart. God is holy because He is like no other, and He exists eternally as the Holy Spirit. God's holiness includes His moral perfection and righteousness. Persons, places, and things set apart for God are holy rather than common.

The incomparable holiness of God is celebrated throughout the Bible, such as in the Song of Moses and the Prayer of Hannah (Ex 15:11; 1 Sm 2:2). The psalms ring with His holiness. His name or character is to be recognized by all others as holy: "For the High and Exalted One who lives forever, whose name is Holy says this: 'I live in a high and holy place, and with the oppressed and lowly of spirit, to revive the spirit of the lowly and revive the heart of the oppressed'" (Is 57:15). Because God is holy, His promises must certainly be fulfilled and His judgment against everything unholy is sure (Ps 89:35; Am 4:2).

God is unsearchable and past finding out, inspiring awe and fear. When humans are confronted with God's holiness, their own unholiness is the more clearly realized, as in the case of Isaiah (Is 6:1-7). All this stands in tension with the personal dimension of God as one seeking to relate to His creatures. God's holiness (which separates Creator from creation) and His personhood (which makes fellowship possible between the Creator and His creatures) are equally true.

The Book of Leviticus in particular focuses on holiness. God ordered the Israelites to set themselves apart from everything ritually or morally profane: "I am the LORD your God, so you must consecrate yourselves and be holy because I am holy" (Lv 11:44). The Apostle Peter applied this text to God's new people (1 Pt 1:15-16). See the article on sanctification for more about the holiness of persons.

Because Jesus is fully divine, He has the same holiness that is attributed to God (Lk 1:35; Jn 6:69). Although God's Spirit worked throughout the Old Testament, He was rarely called the "Holy" Spirit until the birth of Jesus. In Acts and the Epistles, the Spirit gives spiritual life to those who once were unholy and hostile to God. The Holy Spirit lives in all believers, to enable both holy living and good works (Rm 8:9). Christians are frequently called holy ones or saints.

Because God is holy, He will not tolerate ungodliness forever. Divine holiness means that judgment of sin is necessary. God will render a final verdict for all humanity. Everything unholy will be condemned and there will be a new and perfectly holy creation. Peter wrote that "based on His promise, we wait for new heavens and a new earth, where righteousness will dwell" (2 Pt 3:13).

REFLECTION: In what circumstances have you learned the most about God's holiness? What are the personal implications in your life for God's command, "Be holy because I am holy"?

PRAYER: Lord God, You are holy and awesome. Thank You that You exist forever in the Person of the Holy Spirit. Let me become so engulfed by this truth that I am compelled to become more holy. I long for the unfolding of the new creation in which holiness will dwell eternally. Amen.

3.Sovereignty

Riches and honor come from You, and You are the ruler of everything. In Your hand are power and might, and it is in Your hand to make great and to give strength to all. Now therefore, our God, we give You thanks and praise Your glorious name. 1 Chronicles 29:12-13

DEFINITION: God's sovereignty includes both His power to do all that He wills and His rightful exercise of authority over His creation and His creatures. As the Almighty, His rule is righteous, and He expects human beings to recognize and submit to His lordship.

In the language of classic Christian teaching, God's power is called His *omnipotence.* Whatever He wills surely comes to pass. After the New Testament period, the earliest Christian confession (the Apostles' Creed) opened with the words, "I believe in God the Father Almighty, Maker of heaven and earth." Biblical teaching and Christian belief always and everywhere have declared the twin truths that God has all power and that He rules actively as universal Sovereign.

The Old Testament used various names for God, most of which underscore His rule as Lord, both of the world and of Israel. The following list shows the most important of these. The translation is that of the Holman Christian Standard Bible. Other English versions are similar.

Hebrew Original	English Translation
Adonai	Lord
Elohim	God
Yahweh (YHWH)	LORD
Adonai Yahweh	Lord GOD
Yahweh Sabaoth	LORD of Hosts
El Shaddai	God Almighty

In Scripture, *adonai* was also used for the human master in a master-servant relationship (Ex 21:1-6). Since the same term is applied to the God-human relationship, this shows His authority and the duty of His people joyfully to submit to Him. This master-servant bond was reciprocal. On one hand, the servant was to obey the Lord absolutely. On the other hand the Master obligated Himself to care for His servants. Those who called on God by His name, Lord, expected Him to take care of them, and God in turn expected their obedience in all things.

When the New Testament quotes the Old, the Greek *kyrios* (Lord) translates both **Adonai** and **Yahweh.** A striking example is the quotation of Psalm 110:1 in Mark 12:36: "The Lord [Hebrew *Yahweh;* Greek *kyrios*] declared to my Lord [Hebrew *Adonai;* Greek *kyrios*], 'Sit at My right hand until I put Your enemies under Your feet.'" Thus, when Jesus' followers addressed Him as Lord, this meant much more than "master" in an earthly sense. Paul wrote that someday everyone will bow to Jesus and all will "confess that Jesus Christ is Lord, to the glory of God the Father" (Php 2:11). Hence Old Testament belief regarding God's authority was recognized as fully resident in Christ. The New Testament term "master" (Greek *despotes,* from which the English term "despot" comes), used infrequently, referred either to a human master or to God as the sovereign Master (Lk 2:29; Ac 4:24; 2 Tm 2:21; 2 Pt 2:1; Jd 4; Rv 6:10).

REFLECTION: What is the distinction between God's absolute power and His right to exercise authority? Do you agree that it is your duty "joyfully to submit to Him"? Why or why not?

PRAYER: *Sovereign Lord, I acknowledge Your mighty power and wonderful rule over all things. I gladly submit to You and praise You that You care for me, Your willing servant. Amen.*

4. Omniscience

He counts the number of the stars; He gives names to all of them. Our Lord is great, vast in power; His understanding is infinite.

Psalm 147:4-5

DEFINITION: Omniscience means to know all things, and the Scriptures affirm that God alone is all knowing. Although this includes factual knowledge, the biblical emphasis concerns God's intimate knowledge of persons.

The sovereignty of God necessarily implies that He knows everything, down to the smallest details. He knows the number of hairs as well as stars (Lk 12:7). God's omniscience has proven to be a great comfort to believers. One of the outstanding Bible promises can be true only if God is both omnipotent and omniscient: "We know that all things work together for the good of those who love God: those who are called according to His purpose" (Rm 8:28). Several objections to the biblical teaching have been raised. These are listed as questions below, with a brief answer following.

If God knows everything, how could He then regret or repent of certain actions, as in Genesis 6:6 or 1 Samuel 15:35? While nothing that happens ever comes to God as a surprise, this does not mean He is incapable of emotions or reaction against evil. He expresses both grief and wrath against sin because of His love (Eph 4:30).

If Jesus is fully God and God is omniscient, how could Jesus not know certain things, such as the time of His return, as in Mark 13:32? During the period between His birth in Bethlehem and His crucifixion, Jesus emptied Himself and humbled Himself (Php 2:7-8). Evidently during those days He voluntarily gave up the independent use of certain divine attributes. What He spoke was only what the Father revealed to Him (Jn 8:28). Only after His resurrection did Jesus claim to have all authority in heaven and earth (Mt 28:18-20).

Does God's omniscience include "what if's" or contingencies? The biblical teaching is that God absolutely knows what persons would have done even under different circumstances. Jesus criticized the people of Capernaum with these words: "If the miracles that were done in you had been done in Sodom, it would have remained until today" (Mt 11:23).

Does God's omniscience include His knowledge of choices people haven't yet made? Some Bible students (calling themselves "open theists") have recently been answering this question with a no, arguing that God knows everything knowable, but that He does not know the free choices of moral beings because these choices do not yet exist. Classic Christianity has always answered with a resounding yes. To argue otherwise means that prophecies in the Scriptures are only probabilities that might not happen.

God's knowledge of the inner life of His children is especially celebrated in Psalm 139:1-6. Such knowledge, on the other hand, should cause alarm for the unrighteous (Ps 90:8; Pr 15:3; 1 Pt 3:12). God's right to judge mankind in the final judgment includes His knowledge of human secrets (Rm 2:16).

REFLECTION: Does your belief that God knows everything comfort or frighten you? Why? What are the main difficulties people have expressed to you about God's knowledge of all things?

PRAYER: *Lord God, I confess that You know all things. This means that nothing surprises You. I believe that You know me inside and out, so help me to live my life conscious that Your loving but holy eyes are ever upon me. May I live this day in light of my coming judgment. Amen.*

5. Presence

Where can I flee from Your presence? If I go up to heaven, You are there; if I make my bed in Sheol, You are there. If I live at the eastern horizon or settle at the western limits, even there Your hand will lead me.
Psalm 139:7-10

DEFINITION: God's presence is His "being there." Omnipresence means that He is everywhere at all times. There is no place or time God is not. Yet the biblical emphasis is on His manifested presence, experienced only at certain times and places and by specific persons.

One glory of the religion of Israel was that, unlike the deities worshiped by surrounding nations, their Lord was not limited to one geographical location. He was in all places all the time. This is one of the traditional "three omnis" attributed to God. Omnipresence thus takes its place alongside omnipotence (without limit in power) and omniscience (without limit in knowledge). God is without limits—infinite—in space and time as their Creator. All created things and persons are limited to a particular space and time, but not God. Solomon's prayer at the dedication of the temple expressed this fully (2 Ch 6:18). This truth greatly comforts God's people, but is a terror to those who wish to ignore or to hate Him. No escape is possible.

Heaven—the realm beyond earth's atmosphere (with the rain and the birds) and beyond outer space (with the sun and the stars)—is God's home in the sense that His glory is perfectly displayed and adored there, and His will is perfectly obeyed by all who are there: "Your will be done on earth as it is in heaven" (Mt 6:10).

The unseen presence of the Lord in all places and times is assumed throughout the Bible. Yet an experience that revealed His localized presence was what His people longed for. God promised Israel, "I will place My residence among you, and I will not reject you. I will walk among you and be Your God, and you will be My people" (Lv 26:11-12). Both at the tabernacle in the wilderness and at the Jerusalem temple, the people rejoiced that God displayed His presence there (Ex 25:8; 40:34-38; 2 Ch 7:1-3). (In many world religions, a temple is the deity's dwelling, the god's house, and an image or idol was placed there. In Israel's temple such images were forbidden by the Second Commandment. The same is true for Christians.)

Jesus Christ is the localized manifestation of God: "The Word became flesh and took up residence [literally *tabernacled*] among us" (Jn 1:14). One of His names is Immanuel, God With Us. In the Epistles, both the physical body of the individual believer and the body of Christ (the church) are temples for God's very presence (1 Co 3:16; 6:19; 2 Co 6:16; Eph 2:21). One of the terrifying descriptions of eternal punishment is of humans without hope of ever experiencing God's presence: "These will pay the penalty of everlasting destruction, away from the Lord's presence" (2 Th 1:9).

The final state of glory includes the redeemed perfectly experiencing His presence: "Look! God's dwelling is with men, and He will live with them. They will be His people, and God Himself will be with them and be their God" (Rv 21:3).

REFLECTION: How do you distinguish between God's omnipresence and His localized presence? Which one is more important? How have you personally experienced God's presence?

PRAYER: All-present God who ever sees me, I long to experience Your presence this day. Bring me safely to Your heavenly home, where I will dwell in Your presence forever. In the name of Jesus, Immanuel, I pray. Amen.

6. Love

We have come to know and to believe the love that God has for us. God is love, and the one who remains in love remains in God, and God remains in him.... We love because He first loved us.

1 John 4:16,19

DEFINITION: God's love is His freely given, intense affection, actively showing delight and goodwill toward the objects of His pleasure. Grace is His love expressed to those who don't deserve it; mercy is His love shown to those in need.

If contemporary people believe anything at all about God, they believe that He loves. Yet this is often thought of as a kind of vague indulgence, like a forgetful but sentimental grandfather distributing treats. Such a view strips God of His holiness, forgetting that God's wrath and His judgment of evil are also included in His character.

From before the ages began and apart from the creation, God's love has always found perfect expression in the pleasure of the Father, Son, and Spirit for each other. Jesus noted, "The Father loves the Son and has given all things into His hands" (Jn 3:35; see also Jn 14:31). God chose to create, however, and because of His love He cares for His creation providentially. No bird falls from the sky without His concern (Mt 10:29). "The young lions roar for their prey and seek their food from God" (Ps 104:21).

A Christian understanding of God's love focuses on His grace (love expressed toward sinners), and the heart of the gospel is that God in love sent His Son to the world. John 3:16 has become the best known Bible verse with good reason. Although in holiness He cannot overlook evil, in love God invites all humans to repent and believe the gospel. Sinners in rebellion against Him—the world—are the objects of His love.

In yet another sense God's love is directed to His chosen people. He told the Israelites, "The Lord was devoted to you and chose you, not because you were more numerous than all peoples, for you were the fewest of all peoples. But because the Lord loved you and kept the oath He swore to your fathers, He brought you out with a strong hand and redeemed you from the place of slavery" (Dt 7:7-8). This is God's electing love. (See the article on predestination.) The New Testament equivalent is Christ's love for His bride, the church (Eph 5:25). This love resembles the particular love a husband has for his chosen wife, which differs from the general concern he ought to have for other women. God "predestined us to be adopted through Jesus Christ for Himself, according to His favor and will, to the praise of His glorious grace that He favored us with in the Beloved" (Eph 1:5-6).

For His people, God's love is unconditional, but the experience of loving fellowship with Him depends on obedience to His will. Jude 21 exhorts believers to "keep yourselves in the love of God." Jesus Himself declared that obeying His commands was the way to remain in His love (Jn 15:10). "From eternity to eternity the Lord's faithful love is toward those who fear Him ... [and] who remember to observe His instructions" (Ps 103:17-18).

REFLECTION: Why is it essential to see that God's love was perfectly expressed before creation? How have you experienced God's unconditional love? How does obedience relate to God's love?

PRAYER: *Great God of love, You loved the world of undeserving sinners by sending Christ. I praise You because "God is love." Help me to remain in Your love by obeying Your word and seeking to please You in all I am and do. Thank You that Your love lasts forever. Amen.*

7. Trinity

The grace of the Lord Jesus Christ, and the love of God, and the fellowship of the Holy Spirit be with all of you. 2 Corinthians 13:13

DEFINITION: God is eternally one Being. Yet He exists eternally as three Persons, the Father, the Son, and the Spirit. There are not three Gods, only one. The Father, the Son, and the Spirit are distinct from each other.

The term "Trinity" is found nowhere in the Bible, but the biblical foundation for orthodox belief is undeniable. In the earliest centuries of Christianity, a number of challenges by false teachers provoked debate and discussion about the relationship among the Father, the Son, and the Spirit. How should Jesus be understood in relation to the Father? Is there warrant to refer to the Spirit as personal, rather than as a divine force? The Council of Nicea, a notable meeting of Christian leaders in AD 325, published a statement of faith around which true Christians rallied.

What is the relationship of the Son to God? Here's how the framers of the Nicene Creed stated it: "We believe in one Lord, Jesus Christ, the only Son of God, eternally begotten of the Father, God from God, Light from Light, true God from true God, begotten, not made, of one Being with the Father." This reflected the conviction that a number of passages unambiguously refer to Christ as God. An example is Romans 9:5: "From them [the Israelites], by physical descent, came the Messiah, who is God over all, blessed forever. Amen."

Is the Spirit a person? Here's the answer given in the Nicene Creed: "We believe in the Holy Spirit, the Lord, the giver of life, who proceeds from the Father and the Son. With the Father and the Son He is worshiped and glorified." This develops the conviction that the Holy Spirit has emotions or affections, something limited to personal beings. An example is Ephesians 4:30: "And don't grieve God's Holy Spirit, who sealed you for the day of redemption."

The diagram below represents a famous attempt at illustrating the classic conception of the Godhead. Understanding the Trinity has escaped the most brilliant Christian thinkers of the ages, and this doctrine is perhaps best thought of as an inscrutable mystery received by faith.

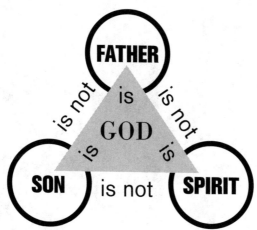

REFLECTION: How does the Trinitarian view of God differ from that of other religions that worship one God? How does this doctrine help explain that God's love existed before creation?

PRAYER: Father, Son, and Spirit, You are wonderful and beyond my ability to understand. I praise You that in the everlasting love of the Persons of the Godhead, You chose to create and to redeem to Yourself other persons to love who will love You in return. Amen.

II.SCRIPTURE

Without a right understanding of the nature of the Bible, the church will cease to exist. Unless God has used His voice understandably, there is no way to know whether Christianity is true. For good reason the word "Word" is applied both to written and speech communication as well as to Jesus Christ, God's personal revelation. "In the beginning was the Word" (Jn 1:1).

Without right interpretation of the Bible, God's voice becomes so muddled that evil persons can manipulate it for evil ends. Even the best of interpreters may confess uncertainty for certain difficult texts. Of course, the question of who has the right to interpret the Bible's message has provoked many a discussion and debate. One factor separating Roman Catholicism from other branches of Christendom is its claim to provide *the* right interpretation of the sacred text, to the exclusion of all who differ. Protestant interpretation has sadly suffered from many, often-contradictory voices that claim, "Thus saith the Lord."

Yet not all is bleak. During the past five centuries, the evangelical consensus about the nature of the Bible has been challenged but not destroyed. Multiplied millions around the world believe the Scripture is the true Word of God. Further, the classic understanding of the main message of the Bible—that which is necessary for the soul's salvation and for safely arriving in the Lord's presence—remains clear. The six studies in this section explore terms related to Scripture that need urgent attention by twenty-first-century followers of Jesus Christ.

8. Inspiration

All Scripture is inspired by God and is profitable for teaching, for rebuking, for correcting, for training in righteousness, so that the man of God may be complete, equipped for every good work.
2 Timothy 3:16-17

DEFINITION: Biblical inspiration refers to the work of the Holy Spirit by which He produced the words of the entire Bible, using the personality and literary skill of its human authors, so that the resultant written text is God's authoritative Word to mankind.

Many works of literature, music, and art have been called inspired, meaning that the author was brilliant. The effect of such work on others is inspiring (moving or inspirational). When Christians refer to the Bible as inspired, they really mean something else, although no doubt the authors of Scripture were brilliant and their work is moving indeed. Biblical inspiration involved both the *processes* by which Scripture was produced and the end *product.*

"Inspiration" comes from a Latin term meaning "to breathe in," referring to God's Spirit at work in the lives of the authors of the Bible. God used a variety of means to reveal Himself to these writers. Moses heard from God directly on Mt. Sinai (Ex 20:1). The Lord said to Isaiah, "I have put My words in your mouth" (Is 51:16). Daniel and others saw visions from God (Dn 7:1). Jesus promised His official ambassadors, the apostles, that the Spirit would guide them into all truth (Jn 16:13). One apostle described the process like this: "No prophecy ever came by the will of man; instead, moved by the Holy Spirit, men spoke from God" (2 Pt 1:21). Inspiration also included such ordinary things as historical research. Luke, for example, introduced his Gospel with the note that he had "carefully investigated everything from the very first" (Lk 1:3).

Thus, on one hand, we refer to the inspired *writers* of Scripture. On the other hand, however, stands the inspired *writing* itself: Scripture, the end result. One reason for believing this distinction comes from noting the words "inspired by God" in 2 Timothy 3:16 cited above. The term in the original is *theopneustos,* meaning "breathed out by God." The Scriptures proceed directly from God's inner self, just as the expulsion of human breath comes from within one's body. The Scriptures could not be more divine if they had been dropped down from God's throne engraved on granite pages. Scriptures are therefore rightly called the Word of God. Careful students of the Bible's inspiration refer to "verbal, plenary inspiration." The term "verbal" refers to the very words of the sacred text, for God not only inspired the *ideas* in the Bible but also the exact *words* required to express the message. The term "plenary" means full. Every bit of Scripture is equally inspired. We do not have the luxury of accepting some parts of the Bible as more inspired than others.

Contemporary interpreters of Scripture, therefore, are never inspired in the sense that the original authors were. Yet we certainly may ask that the same Spirit will *illumine* both the message of Scripture and our own minds to understand the meaning of the inspired text.

REFLECTION: Why believe that the Bible itself (in addition to the Bible writers) is inspired? What is the difference between inspiration and illumination? Have you ever prayed for illumination?

PRAYER: *Spirit of God, You worked in the lives of such persons as Moses, Isaiah, and Paul to bring Your very Word to the world. Thank You for the inspired Word, now available to me. I ask for the same Spirit to illumine me this day to understand the divine message. Amen.*

9. Infallibility

The ordinances of the LORD are reliable and altogether righteous. They are more desirable than gold—than an abundance of pure gold.... In addition, Your servant is warned by them; there is great reward in keeping them.

Psalm 19:9-11

DEFINITION: The infallibility of the Bible means that it is perfectly true and that it accomplishes the purpose the divine Author intended each of its parts to achieve.

The religious and ethical teachings of the Bible declare the mind of God to mankind. He gave His Word not for the joy of theoretical knowledge but to lead persons to know Him, resulting in eternal life. God's Word infallibly performs what He means it to accomplish: "So My word that comes from My mouth will not return to Me empty, but it will accomplish what I please, and will prosper in what I send it to do" (Is 55:11). God's people throughout the ages have depended on Scripture as utterly reliable in at least these ways:

- *Historical accuracy:* The narrative accounts of Scripture that on the surface claim to record real space-time events are in fact accurate descriptions.
- *Scientific facts:* Such facts as the creation of the world and the flood of Noah's time are accepted, not the least because Jesus believed them to be true (Mt 19:4; Lk 17:26-27).
- *Divine commands:* The ethical and religious teachings of the Bible are binding on His people (recognizing that many commands, such as those concerning animal sacrifices, had a built-in obsolescence; Hb 8:13).
- *Prophetic revelation:* The prophecies of the Bible will certainly come to pass. The focus of prophecy is on the first and second coming of the Messiah.

Infallibility, of course, presumes that the Bible is interpreted correctly. Both fools and those who are willfully perverse can twist Scripture so that its message is missed. This goes all the way back to Eden, with the tempter's insinuation, "Did God really say...?" (Gn 3:1). The burden of right interpretation is balanced by the parallel truth of Scripture's *perspicuity* (clarity). This means that Scripture is sufficiently clear in its essential teaching. All believers may read and study it, confident that they will learn all they need for becoming more Christlike.

In the twentieth century, many North American Christians emphasized the term "inerrancy" in their descriptions of the Bible. This term focuses on historical and scientific statements in the Bible as being without error. Because the Bible's religious teachings are often based on the reliability of historical reports (such as the bodily resurrection of Jesus), it is important to insist that these have been accurately recorded. When all the facts have become known, the Bible time and time again has been seen as entirely true. One of the best approaches for understanding inerrancy and infallibility is to study the way Jesus treated the Scriptures of His day. He considered Scripture to be historically accurate, prophetically reliable, and a true record of the will of God. Along these lines He stated, "Scripture cannot be broken" (Jn 10:35) and "You are deceived, because you don't know the Scriptures or the power of God" (Mt 22:29).

REFLECTION: Why believe that the Bible itself is inerrant? What is the difference between infallibility and inerrancy? What are the implications if the Bible is 100-percent true?

PRAYER: Dear Lord, thank You that according to Hebrews 4:12 "the word of God is living and effective and sharper than any two-edged sword, penetrating as far as to divide soul, spirit, joints, and marrow." Help me to live by Your Word today and every day. Amen.

10. The Law

For no flesh will be justified in His sight by the works of the law, for through the law comes the knowledge of sin.   Romans 3:20

DEFINITION: Although the five books of Moses–and the Old Testament as a whole–may be called the Law, in essence " law" refers to all the righteous demands of God that reveal His holy commandments for His people, including moral, religious, and civil obligations.

Because "law" is used in such a variety of contexts in the Bible, it has been widely misunderstood. The easiest level is to recognize that Genesis through Deuteronomy are the books of the Law (*torah* in Hebrew), and the Jewish Scriptures can then be called "the Law and the Prophets" (Mt 7:12; 11:13; 22:40; Ac 13:15; 28:33; Rm 3:21). Sometimes the entire biblical revelation before Christ's coming is called the law (Rm 3:19).

In the sense of "commandments" (comprising all the moral, religious, and civil requirements God asked the Israelites to obey), it must be understood above all that the law was never given as a means of salvation, even though some first-century Jews (and many in other centuries) misapplied the law in this way. The Ten Commandments, for example, were given to those already redeemed from slavery. Further, these requirements were a temporary tutor between the time of Moses and the coming of Christ, as Paul explained in Galatians 3:23-25. The author of Hebrews noted that Mosaic law was superseded now that the new covenant has been established (Hb 8:7-13). Whatever believers in Christ make of the law commands in Scripture, they ought never to suppose that good works or keeping God's laws can earn salvation or divine favor, and they must keep in mind that all ceremonial regulations (such as rules for sacrifice) have been fulfilled and ended through Jesus Christ.

Many Christian thinkers have discerned three legitimate ongoing uses of the law for God's people today. Thoughtful reflection reveals the following:

- *The mirror function.* On one hand, the moral laws of the Bible (including those in the New Testament) reveal God's perfect holiness. On the other hand, by these same laws comes the knowledge of sin and conviction of the need for the gospel and grace. Paul especially taught this in Romans 7:7-12. Once one learns from a mirror that one's face is unclean (*by the law*) then the proper cleansing remedy can be applied (*by the gospel*).

- *The civil function.* The moral laws of God applied by governments restrain evil to a degree. Even though applying such law cannot change hearts, threats of punishment may secure order in society and protect the innocent from the guilty, as in Romans 13:3-4. (The church as an institution may only warn or excommunicate violators of civil commands.)

- *The guide function.* For those whom God has regenerated, the law is a "yardstick" showing growth in good works and Christlikeness. Jesus said, "If you love Me, you will keep My commandments" (Jn 14:15). Galatians 6:2 and James 1:25 reflect this truth, and Psalm 119 is a ringing anthem about the greatness of God's law: "How happy are those whose way is blameless, who live according to the law of the LORD" (Ps 119:1).

REFLECTION: When did you first realize that the law could not save anyone? How intentionally do you use the moral teachings of the Bible as a guide to measure your growth in holiness?

PRAYER: *Lord God, Your law is wonderful and good, even though it reveals me to be a miserable sinner. I bless You for Your Spirit's help aiding me to grow in obeying Your moral laws. Amen.*

11. Prophecy

You may say to yourself, "How can we recognize a message the LORD has not spoken?" When a prophet speaks in the LORD's name, and the message does not come true or is not fulfilled, that is a message the LORD has not spoken. Deuteronomy 18:21-22

DEFINITION: Prophets were spokesmen for God, with a message inspired by His Spirit that often included predictions about near and remote events. Their prophecies, given orally at first, were often written down and included in the Scriptures.

When Elijah confronted the people of Israel at Mt. Carmel concerning their worship of Baal, he became the prototype for understanding the essence of biblical prophecy (1 Kg 18). The prophets who preceded Elijah mainly functioned as inside supporters of Israel's religion and leaders (Moses, Samuel, and Nathan come to mind). After Elijah, the prophets mainly were outsiders, independent of Israel's kings and priests and challengers of the status quo (Isaiah, Jeremiah, and Ezekiel come to mind). The typical prophetic confrontation began with a stern, "thus saith the Lord," a phrase found more than 400 times in the familiar King James Version.

The main function of biblical prophecy therefore was to "forthtell" the mind of God concerning His holiness. The prophets expressed the Lord's longing for His people to order their moral and spiritual lives around what He valued. The independent prophets were often scorned and their writings were even burned (Jr 36:27). Yet some of them left writings that survived, and these were collected, so that Israel's Scripture came to be called "the Law and the Prophets."

God was pleased to reveal certain coming events to the prophets. A secondary function of biblical prophecy was to "foretell." Often these events occurred in the prophet's lifetime, and this proved that the Lord was truly speaking through the prophet (as cited in Dt 18:21-22 above). Thus, Isaiah predicted to King Hezekiah that the Assyrian invasion under Sennacherib would fail and that Jerusalem would be spared (Isaiah 37). This function continued during the early Christian period as well, for example, Agabus's prophecy of a coming famine (Ac 11:28). Jesus' prophecy of Jerusalem's fall, fulfilled in AD 70, may also fit this category (Mt 24:2).

The second kind of prophetic prediction foresaw events that lay beyond the prophet's lifetime. These remote prophecies centered on the coming of Israel's Messiah. That there would be two comings of the Messiah, separated by thousands of years, was not plainly revealed to them. The light of the New Testament makes this clear. For example, Isaiah 53 certainly prophesied Jesus' death as the Suffering Servant, while Isaiah 65–66 speaks of the final glory that will be.

Right interpretation of biblical prophecy, then, requires paying careful attention. First, we must distinguish between moral or spiritual counsel (forthtelling) and prediction (foretelling). Second, we must remember the three settings that are possible for predictions, as noted below.

FIRST SETTING	SECOND SETTING	THIRD SETTING
NEAR PROPHECY	REMOTE PROPHECY	ULTIMATE PROPHECY
The Prophet's Lifetime	Messiah's First Coming	Messiah's Second Coming

REFLECTION: Which kind of prophecy is more important, forthtelling or foretelling? Why? How important is it for Christians to study the Old Testament prophetic books?

PRAYER: God of the prophets, thank You for Your word that came through such inspired men as Isaiah and Jeremiah. Help me to hear through them any "thus saith the Lord" to which I need to respond. Help me live this day in honor of the Messiah the prophets proclaimed. Amen.

12. Interpretation

Then He opened their minds to understand the Scriptures.
Luke 24:45

DEFINITION: To interpret a passage of Scripture is to explain its message: first as it was meant to be understood in its original setting; and second as it has significance in a contemporary setting. Christ is the central theme of Scripture, and the Spirit guides persons to right interpretation.

Every written document has to be interpreted, from a daily newspaper to the United States *Constitution* to Shakespeare's *Macbeth*. For all documents—whether they are of great historical value or as personal as a grocery list—the first goal is to discover what the original author intended by his or her written message. So it is with the Bible. The primary task is to determine, as nearly as possible, what a passage meant. For this reason, it's important to study such matters as historical background and literary types (such as poetry and parables). Only then can a passage be applied, because a biblical text cannot *mean* today something contrary to what it *meant* originally. (For example, Acts 5:32-37 can't be used to teach that all Christians should sell their real estate and give it to church leaders unless one first shows that the author was giving a universal prescription rather than a historical description.)

Much has been said about "literal" interpretation. This means that words are taken in their ordinary literary and historical sense, taking into account figures of speech and other such devices. Thus when a historical narrative records, for example, that the Israelites left Egypt under Moses' leadership, literal interpreters believe that there was a real human figure named Moses and a literal event referred to as the exodus. Yet when John in a vision saw Jesus with a sword coming from His mouth, we understand this to be figurative, a symbol of His powerful word.

Biblical interpretation centers on Jesus Christ and is enabled by the Spirit of Christ working in the lives of earnest believers who humbly request the Spirit's illumination. Because Scripture is internally cohesive, a great principle of interpretation is that "Scripture is its own best interpreter." Others refer to this as "the analogy of Scripture." A parallel principle is "the analogy of faith," that is, the consensus of devout interpreters through the centuries. As noted in the introduction to this book, such harmony has been expressed in the creeds affirmed by all Christians everywhere and in the five great Reformation principles.

All believers are responsible to interpret for themselves, aided by godly preachers and teachers. The Bible is sufficiently clear in itself for the typical believer, equipped with basic principles of interpretation, to learn the message of Scripture. Yet highly trained biblical scholars will be able to interpret more fully than others, pointing to the need for formally educated church leaders. What happens when sincere Christians disagree, inevitable once one has abandoned the idea of an infallible human interpreter? If the interpretation rejects a matter central to the gospel, then it is to be rejected as unorthodox or heretical. If the explanation falls within "the analogy of faith," then Christian charity requires one to withhold criticism more severe than saying, "In my judgment, this interpretation is in error, but it is within the bounds of orthodoxy."

REFLECTION: Why does every written document have to be interpreted? How important is it to seek to discover what a Bible passage meant in its original context?

PRAYER: Lord, help me to be diligent in my quest to understand the Word, as one who longs to know its message aright so that I may live by its life-giving light. In Christ's name I pray. Amen.

13. Great Commandments

Love the Lord your God with all your heart, with all your soul, and with all your mind. This is the greatest and most important commandment. The second is like it: Love your neighbor as yourself. All the Law and the Prophets depend on these two commandments.

Matthew 22:37-40

DEFINITION: The Great Commandments are Jesus' summary of the religious and moral message of the Scriptures of His day, and the New Testament shows their expanded application. Christians live by these two overarching principles not only in this life but also for eternity.

When Jesus and the Pharisees clashed, it wasn't because they disagreed about treating Scripture as God's Word. It was that Jesus rejected Pharisee traditions that had no basis in Scripture (Mt 15:1-9). Further, Jesus was radical in His approach to Scripture in the true sense of the word "radical," that is, "pertaining to the root or foundation of something" (from the Latin *radix*, root). Jewish biblical scholars had organized all the commands of Scripture into neat lists, but evidently they disagreed about whether one command was greater than any other. When they confronted Jesus with their dilemma, He famously answered with the Great Commandments. And by "love" Jesus meant "delight, devotion, value, and esteem."

Why are the Great Commandments so admirable? First, consider how well they summarize the Ten Commandments. Love for God (Dt 6:4-5) is the focus of commandments 1–4. The last six commandments describe ways to show love for fellow humans (Lv 19:18). Second, consider that Jesus' life showed how to live in perfect compliance with these two laws. Third, consider that all the spiritual and moral guidelines of the New Testament can be summarized under these headings. Finally, these commands show that in the truest sense there is no incompatibility between love and obedience.

Why is love for God put above all other commands? The answer, of course, is that He is supremely lovely and lovable. No one else is as wise and wonderful and great and good and beautiful as Almighty God. Therefore, it is inconceivable that He should ask any of His creatures to love anyone else supremely. To do so would ask them to put the highest value on what does not have the highest value. And whenever they love someone else supremely, it is idolatry.

Why is love for one's fellow human beings placed second only to love for God? Because humans alone of all God's creation were made in His image (Gn 1:27). Every human life (preborn or near death; sick or healthy; moral or wicked) has value because it bears the divine stamp—however marred—and will live forever, either in misery or in bliss.

About things of eternal value, Paul wrote, "Now these three remain: faith, hope, and love. But the greatest of these is love" (1 Co 13:13). Thus, those who learn love in this life are simply practicing how they will live eternally. Yet love in this life can never be absolutely perfect because of the effects of sin that still mar our present existence. In heaven, love will increase forever, undimmed by the presence of sin. Then we will experience the full enjoyment of loving God and our fellows with none of the complications that attend love in the present.

REFLECTION: How conscious are you on a daily basis that you are living with love for God and for others? What steps could you take to be more deliberate in this regard?

PRAYER: Lord God, I love You, but not as much as I ought. I want to grow in loving You this very day. I desire to grow in delight, devotion, value, and esteem for my fellow humans as well. And help me to love someone today whom I do not naturally value. In Jesus' name, amen.

III.CREATION (AND MANKIND)

The Eighth Psalm celebrates the intricate vastness of the universe God made as well as mankind's splendor as the pinnacle of creation. "You ... crowned him [man] with glory and honor. You made him lord over the works of Your hands" (Ps 8:5-6). Christians have always and everywhere believed that God created everything. The Apostles' Creed begins, "I believe in God the Father Almighty, Maker of heaven and earth." The Bible doesn't argue scientifically for an "Intelligent Designer" of the world anymore than it provides philosophical arguments for His existence. The approach of the Scriptures toward such things is announced in the opening words, "In the beginning, God created ..." (Gn 1:1).

As the biblical story unfolds after the first verse, we find startling claims both about the kind of world God created and about the nature of the personal moral beings within it. Surely to understand the nature of our own race—created in God's image, and blessed with male-female marriage from the first—is vital. This is so because in today's secularized culture, not every human life is treasured. Further, challenges to the traditional understanding of marriage are threatening to undo the social arrangement that has provided great stability for both home and nation, throughout the world, but especially in the historically Christianized countries.

Follow the seven studies in this section to come to a better understanding of the historic and biblical teaching on these important concepts. Every Christ-follower should be able to answer the question the psalmist asked of God, "When I observe Your heavens ... what is man that You remember him?" (Ps 8:3-4).

14.Image of God

Then God said, "Let Us make man in Our image, according to Our likeness. They will rule the fish of the sea, the birds of the sky, the animals, all the earth, and the creatures that crawl on the earth."

Genesis 1:26

DEFINITION: Human beings resemble God in that they have personality, morality, and spirituality; further, they represent God as His agent to the animals and the rest of creation. Although sin has marred the image of God in everyone except Christ, the image is not destroyed.

The Bible never defines precisely the image of God (*imago Dei* in Latin), so this important concept has received close attention. The Old Testament term "image" could be translated "representation," and many of its instances in fact refer to idols as images of a person or animal (Ezk 7:20). The Old Testament term "likeness" implies comparison—explaining one thing by relating it to another. Thus mankind may be partly understood by looking at God. (If the comparison went the other direction, we would say that God is the image of man—and the Bible is full of warnings not to reduce God to man's idea of Him; Is 40:18.)

The *personality* aspect of mankind's bearing the likeness of God includes both intellect and affections. Intelligence, rationality, and the ability to think are other terms used to describe intellect. The affections—understood more broadly than the usual term "emotions"—include feelings and determination, but not merely "bodily passions," such as pain and appetite, which are limited to physically induced feelings. The affections move one to act, and both God and the angels (without bodily existence) are endowed with such affections. Thus both God and mankind may set their love on specific objects or persons. *Because God is love, mankind may love as well* (1 Jn 4:16).

The *morality* of mankind means the ability to choose what is right. God's perfect holiness (righteousness) means that He always does what is right. Mankind's fall into sin means that our moral "chooser" is broken so that we are apt to choose that which is morally evil rather than that which is morally good. Salvation includes persons receiving new hearts that will freely choose God and good, ultimately resulting in the holiness of all the saints in heaven. *Because God is holy, mankind may be holy as well* (1 Pt 1:15-16).

Spirituality includes the ability to relate intimately to others face-to-face. God exists in the perfect relationship of the Persons of the Trinity; human beings may know each other—and they may know and be known by God. Further, "spirit" or "soul" refers to that component of a human surviving bodily death. *Because God is spirit, mankind has spiritual capacity as well* (Jn 4:24).

The *representation* aspect of mankind as God's likeness means that to the animal world (and the rest of the created order), man has a Godlike role. This function of humanity's rule over the creation has continued since mankind's fall into sin, although often in a distorted way. For example, the only "God" that pets or wildlife experience is their master or tamer.

REFLECTION: How essential is it to believe that every human life bears God's image? How does knowing that you bear His image affect your connection to Him? To other persons? To animals?

PRAYER: Eternal God, thank You for giving me the privilege of bearing Your image. And forgive me for the times I willfully distort that image as I relate to You and to others. Help me respect every human being I encounter as worthy of honor for also bearing Your image. Amen.

15. Angels

Then war broke out in heaven: Michael and his angels fought against the dragon. The dragon and his angels also fought, but he could not prevail, and there was no place for them in heaven any longer.

Revelation 12:7-8

DEFINITION: An angel is one of the multitudes of personal supernatural spirit beings that God made. All angels were created good, but some fell into evil. In English, "angel" is derived directly from the Greek *angelos,* meaning "messenger," one function of certain good angels.

Various cultural and religious traditions about angels have developed over many centuries. The biblical information is limited and mysterious. Angels often served as mighty warriors carrying out divine judgment against evil, such as destroying Sodom or killing an Assyrian army (Gn 19:1; 2 Ch 32:21). Sometimes they aided God's people (Ex 23:23), and the fiery chariots and horses that Elijah and Elisha saw were evidently angel armies, or the heavenly host (2 Kg 2:11; 6:17). "The angel of the LORD," mentioned about fifty times in the Old Testament, may have been a manifestation of the Son of God before He became flesh.

Cherubs are winged angels related especially to the glorious presence of God. Carved representations of cherubs sat atop the Israelites' sacred ark (Num 7:89; Ezk 10:1-22). Isaiah saw six-winged seraphs ("burning ones"), perhaps the same as the living creatures described by Ezekiel and John (Is 6:1-7; Ezk 1:4-21; Rv 4:6-8). Gabriel and Michael are the only holy angels named in Scripture. (Evil angels are discussed more fully in the articles on the Devil and on demons.)

Angels surrounded the life of Jesus, especially His birth and His resurrection. Angels are prominently associated with Christ's return both in the Gospels and in Revelation. They are sometimes described as men wearing white or dazzling clothes (Mk 16:5; Ac 1:10). Aside from the living creatures of Revelation, no New Testament angelic creature is described as having wings. Angels number in the multiplied thousands (Rv 5:11).

A number of New Testament persons received divine messages from angels (examples: Mary, Lk 1:26-38; shepherds, Lk 2:9-15; women at the tomb, Mt 28:2-7; Philip, Ac 8:26; and Paul, Ac 27:23). On occasion they did mighty acts on behalf of believers or as agents of divine judgment (Ac 12:7-11,23). As the citation of Revelation 12:7-8 above shows, good angels and evil angels oppose each other in supernatural spiritual warfare (see Eph 6:12).

Jesus taught that angels have a special relationship to children and that they do not marry, presumably because they are asexual (Mt 18:10; 22:30). Paul warned against emphasizing angels (Col 2:18). He also hinted that angels are highly organized and taught that believers will someday judge angels (Eph 3:10; 1 Co 6:3). Hebrews teaches more about angels than any other epistle, and chapters 1 and 2 are especially concerned to show the superiority of Christ to angels. Although there is no direct biblical teaching that humans have guardian angels, they are "ministering spirits sent out to serve those who are going to inherit salvation" (Hb 1:14).

REFLECTION: To what extent are your beliefs about angels based on Scripture? On popular culture? Would you accept as valid the claims of someone who supposedly saw an angel?

PRAYER: Holy Father, You created angels to be Your servants. They are mighty and they are Your messengers. They also mysteriously serve those who will be finally redeemed. Thank You that the Lord Jesus, Your eternal uncreated Son, is superior to all angels. Amen.

16.Miracles

Men of Israel, listen to these words: This Jesus the Nazarene was a man pointed out to you by God with miracles, wonders, and signs that God did among you through Him, just as you yourselves know.

Acts 2:22

DEFINITION: A miracle is a powerful intervention worked by God or some other supernatural agent in which ordinary operations (the laws of nature) are displaced, often serving as public signs authenticating the human agent through whom the miracle is performed.

Enlightenment thinkers of the eighteenth century argued that everything could be understood by human reason and that the entire universe must be explained scientifically through the laws of cause and effect. There was no place in this system for miracles, which imply that something beyond natural law can be at work. Christian thinkers responded with a variety of defenses for miracles as truly God-caused events. C. S. Lewis's book *Miracles* was the most popular twentieth-century work defending both the idea and the actual occurrence of miracles.

Careful use of the term "miracle" must be distinguished from casual use. In the truest sense, none of the following classify as a miracle.

- A magnificent sight (mountains, seas, starry sky). Such is nature, not miracle.
- An awe-inspiring event (baby's birth, falling in love). Such is providence, not miracle.
- Most answers to prayer. Such do not usually have sign value confirming an agent as divine.
- Spiritual transformation in someone's life. This is usually not externally discernable.

- Magic or sleight of hand, in which the illusionist knows how to pull off the trick.

The Bible, moreover, gives examples of miraculous deeds done by the Devil and his agents (Mt 24:24; 2 Th 2:9; Rv 13:14). If the exorcisms of Jesus are counted as miracles, then the original demonic possession must equally be counted as a miracle of darkness.

The miracles reported in the Bible focus on—but are not limited to—three time periods. In all cases, the miraculous deeds served to authenticate the human agent. These periods are the time of Moses the lawgiver (and his successor Joshua); Elijah the great prophet (and his successor Elisha); and Jesus the Savior (and His successors the apostles). Christian thinking has disagreed whether workers of divine and supernatural miracles should be expected today.

Jesus' miracles impacted three realms, and their sign value is always clear (people recognized that God had intervened). These three are: (1) the supernatural realm (the exorcisms or casting out demons, showing Jesus' authority over evil spirits); (2) the realm of human bodies (the healings, showing Jesus' compassion); and (3) the realm of nature (the nature miracles, such as the feeding of the 5,000). Jesus refused to do miracles on demand, and He knew that a faith based on miracles is inadequate. The two grand miracles, stupendous signs indeed, are the incarnation and the resurrection of Christ (Jn 1:14; Rm 1:4). Jesus' miracles pointed to His identity as Messiah, but the resurrection alone proved He is God's Son.

REFLECTION: Have you heard people use the term "miracle" carelessly? Why should the word be used carefully? To what extent do you think divine miracles are being done in today's world?

PRAYER: Lord God of miracles, thank You for the greatest of all Your mighty deeds, sending Your Son in human flesh, and raising Him from the dead as proof that He is truly the Son of God, our Lord and Savior. Amen.

17. Marriage

"Haven't you read," He [Jesus] replied, *"that He who created them in the beginning **made them male and female,** and He also said: **For this reason a man will leave his father and mother and be joined to his wife, and the two will become one flesh?** So they are no longer two but one flesh. Therefore what God has joined together, man must not separate."*   Matthew 19:4-6

DEFINITION: Marriage, a God-given institution, is a legally recognized relationship, made formal by a civil or religious ceremony, between one man and one woman, who commit to live together in maintaining a home, to share sexual intimacy, and (usually) to bear and rear children.

Marriage is the most pervasive of institutions, found in every culture known to humanity. Bible students have often noted that this is the only human institution ordained by God before mankind's fall into sin. One man and one woman for life—as in the case of Adam and Eve—is clearly the standard. The Bible provides numerous examples of marriages that failed to meet the divine ideal stated in Genesis 1. Polygamy and no-fault or easy divorce are sad illustrations. The seventh of the Ten Commandments, "Do not commit adultery" (Ex 20:14), shows the great value God places on the sanctity of marriage. Although a number of Old Testament characters practiced polygamy, the New Testament reaffirms the original ideal, for example in the lists of qualifications for leaders in Christian congregations (1 Tm 3:2-12).

Recent decades have witnessed an explosion of couples publicly cohabiting without the benefit or intention of marrying. This used to be called "living in sin," and it is still an apt description for those who treat sexual intimacy casually and who flaunt the divine standard. Similarly, but even more recently, same-sex couples have become much more public about their domestic situation. Some civil jurisdictions have legalized marriages between such persons, but those who read the Bible seriously would have to agree that the only explicit scriptural references to marriage are heterosexual. Further, there is no biblical passage that speaks favorably about homosexual activity. (See Rm 1:26-27 for the most extensive New Testament treatment of the topic.)

Jesus' teaching that we must not separate what God has joined must be taken with all seriousness among Christian marriage partners. Recent surveys show that the divorce rate among North American Christians is virtually identical to society in general. This is cause for great sorrow and alarm, for at least two reasons. First, it shows that the biblical teaching on the permanence of marriage has not been adequately taught (and grasped) within congregational life. Second, this makes it difficult to maintain Paul's teaching that marriage illustrates Christ's unconditional and permanent love for His church, His bride (Eph 5:25-33). This same passage shows that the proper role of a Christian husband is to love his wife sacrificially, to respect her, and to lead the home. The role of a Christian wife is to respond to her husband's love in joyful cooperation, to respect him, and to preserve the home.

REFLECTION: Why is it important to recognize marriage as a God-given institution? What difference does a marriage ceremony make, after all? Why do you think it is so difficult to use the language "living in sin" to describe cohabiting couples?

PRAYER: Lord Christ, one reason marriage was made was to picture Your relationship to Your Church. Yours was the plan that made a man and a woman to live together. May I live in such a way that I honor Your divine intentions for marriage. Amen.

18. Covenants

Then God said to Noah and his sons with him, "Understand that I am confirming My covenant with you and your descendants after you.... The bow will be in the clouds, and I will look at it and remember the everlasting covenant." Genesis 9:8-9,16

DEFINITION: A covenant (*berith* in Hebrew) is a binding agreement between two parties. The scriptural focus is on covenants initiated by God, for which He provided visible signs and for which He sometimes attached stipulations or conditions.

Among North Americans, the language of covenant is largely unused. The idea of marriage as a covenant still persists (with a ring as a visible sign). In some neighborhoods, homeowners must sign a covenant concerning their obligations about property maintenance and appearance. Similar ideas were found in biblical human-to-human covenants, such as the covenant of friendship between David and Jonathan (1 Sm 18:3-4) or the treaty Joshua made with the people of Gibeon (Jos 9:15). Marriage as a covenant is referred to in Malachi 2:14.

The greater interest of the Bible is on covenants that God established with mankind. The earliest account is God's covenant with Noah and the whole human race after the flood in Genesis 9. God as the Sovereign initiated the terms of the agreement: He pledged Himself to send no more worldwide flood; no human condition was given. Further, He stated a visible sign of the covenant, the rainbow.

Four other biblical covenants are even more prominent.

1. The covenant with Abraham. God unconditionally chose Abraham to be a channel of worldwide blessing (fulfilled by Christ) and promised to make from him and his wife Sarah a great nation of biological descendents (Gn 15:1-20). Abraham's response was faith (Gn

15:6). The sign of the Abrahamic covenant is male circumcision (Gn 17:1-22).

2. The covenant at Mt. Sinai. God entered into a conditional covenant with the Israelites at Mt. Sinai when He gave the law (Dt 5:1-22). He promised to bless obedience and to curse disobedience. According to Hebrews 8:13, this covenant was meant to be temporary. The sign of the Sinaitic covenant is the Sabbath, resting on the seventh day of each week (Dt 5:12-15).

3. The covenant with David. God unconditionally chose David to be the first in an ongoing dynasty of kings to rule over God's people (2 Sm 7:1-29). The sign of this covenant is for a Davidic king to be reigning. Jesus is the ultimate fulfillment of this covenant, which is why the New Testament emphasizes Jesus' proclamation of (and rule over) the kingdom.

4. The new covenant. Jeremiah prophesied the new covenant, in which God's people would be forgiven and would wholly love the Lord from renewed hearts (Jr 31:31-33). When Jesus instituted the Lord's Supper, He spoke of the "new covenant in my blood" (Lk 22:20; 1 Co 11:25). Thus the Lord's Supper (Eucharist or Holy Communion) is the sign of the new covenant. Hebrews 8:8-12 quotes Jeremiah's prophecy at length and then provides an extensive explanation of its meaning (Hb 8–9).

REFLECTION: How do the covenants affect your relationship with God? Why think about covenants as part of Christianity? How does the new covenant affect your view of Communion?

PRAYER: Lord God of the covenants, You are the covenant-making and the covenant-keeping God. Above all I praise You for the new covenant through Jesus Christ the King and Son of David. Help me to live my life in faith, love, hope, and obedience to Him this day. Amen

19. Circumcision

And he [Abraham] received the sign of circumcision as a seal of the righteousness that he had by faith while still uncircumcised. This was to make him the father of all who believe but are not circumcised, so that righteousness may be credited to them also.   Romans 4:11-12

DEFINITION: Physical circumcision refers to the act of cutting off the foreskin of a male's reproductive organ. Spiritual circumcision refers to the inner change by which a person is enabled to trust, love, and obey God wholeheartedly.

In recent times, circumcision has been widely practiced in the Western world as a medical procedure, done for its supposed health benefit later in life for the male and for his sexual partner(s). This practice should be kept entirely separate from the discussion of circumcision as a religious ritual.

In the Bible, circumcision was first a ritual symbolizing the covenant God made with Abraham, and which his male descendants were supposed to practice (Gn 17:14). Later on, circumcision on the eighth day of an Israelite boy's life became mandatory (Lv 12:3). By Paul's time, circumcision was often interpreted by Jews to mean that every circumcised person was automatically right with God. This triggered an early Christian controversy about whether non-Jews who came into a right relationship with God by faith should be circumcised (Ac 15). Was circumcision a good work that contributed to one's standing before God? Paul answered with an emphatic no (Gl 5:1-12; 6:12-15; Rm 2:25-29; 4:10-12).

The Old Testament emphasized the importance of bodily circumcision, yet a few texts pointed to the truth that Israelite circumcision should be considered a sign that one had experienced the inner spiritual cleansing that comes by faith (Dt 10:16; Jr 4:4). Most remarkable is the promise of Deuteronomy 30:6: "The LORD your God will circumcise your heart and the hearts of your descendants, and you will love Him with all your heart and all your soul, so that you will live."

This provided the basis for Paul's argument in Romans 2:25-28 that circumcised persons who misbehave are worse off than uncircumcised men who do the right thing. This climaxed in his amazing announcement that "a person is not a Jew who is one outwardly, and true circumcision is not something visible in the flesh" (Rm 2:28). Following Paul's lead, Christianity has rejected circumcision as a ritual to be practiced by churches: "Circumcision does not matter and uncircumcision does not matter, but keeping God's commandments does" (1 Co 7:19). By *commandments,* Paul obviously meant God's *moral commands* rather than *ceremonial rules,* because circumcision was in fact commanded for all Jews (Lv 12:3). It is of some interest that of the New Testament epistles, circumcision is mentioned only in Paul's letters. Thus, the meaning of circumcision for Christians is found in Paul's advice to the Philippians: "We are the circumcision, the ones who serve by the Spirit of God, boast in Christ Jesus, and do not put confidence in the flesh" (Php 3:3; see Col 2:11).

REFLECTION: Why have Gentile Christians rejected circumcision as a religious ritual? How would you explain the difference between physical circumcision and spiritual circumcision?

PRAYER: *Father of Abraham, thank You that the value of circumcision is that it points to an inner spiritual reality, whether someone is male or female. And help me to live with the same kind of faith that Abraham and Sarah had even before You asked for circumcision. Amen.*

20. Sabbath

Then He [Jesus] told them, "The Sabbath was made for man, and not man for the Sabbath. Therefore the Son of Man is Lord even of the Sabbath."   Mark 2:27-28

DEFINITION: Sabbath (Hebrew *shabbat*) means rest. It refers in particular to resting on the seventh day of the week in obedience to the fourth of the Ten Commandments.

The creation account concluded with God's rest on the seventh day (Gn 2:2). This of course was not because He was tired but evidently because it commemorated the completion of His creative activity. The first account of humans resting on the seventh day of the week is found in Exodus 16:20-31. This established the pattern later set forth in the Law of Moses (Dt 5:12-15). As a sign of God's covenant with Israel made at Mt. Sinai, the Sabbath became a great preaching topic for later prophets. Israelites who worked on the seventh day were showing their rejection of the terms of the covenant (Is. 56:2-6; Jr 17:21-27). After the Babylonian Captivity, the Jewish gathering for worship in synagogues occurred on the seventh day of the week, but the Sabbath still retained its focus as a day of rest.

By the time of Jesus, rabbis had gone to great lengths to define the kinds of activities that were permitted on the Sabbath. Indeed, Jesus infuriated some of the Jewish leaders by doing acts of mercy (healing) on the Sabbath. He insisted that He was Lord of the Sabbath and could therefore determine what Sabbath activity was appropriate (Mk 2:23-26).

After Jesus' resurrection, the first day of the week was immediately established as the right weekday for worshiping the Lord (Jn 20:1,19,26; Ac 20:7; 1 Co 16:2). Nevertheless, Jewish believers continued to rest on the Sabbath. A tiny minority of Gentile believers have continued the practice of worshiping and resting on Saturday, notably Seventh Day Adventists.

Within Christian history, debate has swirled around the issue of whether worship on the first day of the week should also include rest from labor. The English Puritans especially answered with a strong yes. Their teaching influenced North American Christianity for hundreds of years, with most businesses closed on Sundays, but in recent decades the practical answer has been no. (Ask most any minister or church staff member whether they rest on Sunday.)

Some have argued that the Fourth Commandment with its emphasis on rest has completely been fulfilled in Christ and has no direct bearing on today's believers. They point to Colossians 2:16 and Hebrews 4 as evidence. Others believe that the point of the commandment is that one must rest one day a week, but which day is open for personal choice. Perhaps all agree that having a regular day for rest and "recharging" is desirable. Yet there remain major differences in the way Christians interpret the biblical teaching about the Sabbath. The larger issue is to remember that Jesus promised rest for the weary (Mt 11:28). "Let us then make every effort to enter that rest, so that no one will fall into the same pattern of disobedience" (Hb 4:11).

REFLECTION: Does your life reflect to any degree one day a week in which you worship and rest? What do you believe about the ongoing validity of the Fourth Commandment?

PRAYER: Dear Lord of the Sabbath, You have provided rest for my soul, and long ago you provided rest for weary bodies by giving the Sabbath. Help me honor You in the very ways I rest my body, and thank You for the heavenly rest of the saints already in Your presence. Amen.

IV. SIN

The term "sin" has been relegated to the backwaters of public conversation. Failings, weaknesses, illegal activities, and flaws are still permissible for discussion, but not sin. Only the most scandalous of crimes (terrorist activities, for example, or child molestation) even warrant the description "evil." By contrast, the Bible assumes sin on virtually every page. It is the human predicament that Jesus Christ came to remedy. Right away the Christian vocabulary is at odds with the "sin-less" vocabulary of current culture.

Yet what exactly is this quandary that Scripture (and every generation of Christian preachers and thinkers) calls sin? Are people basically good, with sin as an occasional aberration, and the gospel simply the means of getting back on track? On this view, the Bible can function as a self-help manual. Or are human beings basically sinful, prone towards evil, and unable to become truly good apart from Christ? With this perspective, the gospel is good news of God's intervention in Christ. It is help for those unable to help themselves.

Even so, we must ask deeper questions about the sin problem. Has sin merely weakened and sickened the human spirit so that the gospel is like medicine? Or has sin actually deadened the spirit so that it must be given new life? Such issues are explored as we look at the six terms explored in the following section.

21. Original Sin

Therefore, just as sin entered the world through one man, and death through sin, in this way death spread to all men, because all sinned. In fact, sin was in the world before the law, but sin is not charged to one's account when there is no law.   Romans 5:12-13

DEFINITION: When Adam and Eve disobeyed God in the garden of Eden in the fall, their nature was damaged or distorted, and their descendants (all humans after them) have been born in a sinful condition.

Thinking about original sin best occurs in the context of three presuppositions. First, all humans have descended biologically from a single human couple (Adam and Eve). Second, Romans 5, the most extensive New Testament passage on the effects of Adam's sin, makes sense only if there was a historical fall. Third, original sin means that the effects of Adam and Eve's fall into sin are passed from one generation to the next. One way to think about this is that "faulty spiritual DNA" is continually passed down, and parents have no more say about passing on that "DNA" than they do about passing on, say, the DNA for brown eyes.

Original sin is the biblical explanation for why human beings died between the time of Adam and the time of Moses. During that period, nobody violated any specific law of God, because He had not given any such commandments. Why then did people die if death comes only as the wages of sin? Because they were already considered sinners "in Adam." This also at least partly explains why babies die: "through one trespass there is condemnation for everyone" (Rm 5:18).

Original sin as a concept was by no means invented by Paul. David reflected this understanding in his poignant poem: "Indeed, I was guilty when I was born; I was sinful when my mother conceived me" (Ps 51:5). In no way was David suggesting that the sexual activity that brings about conception was itself inherently evil, anymore than that the birth process is sinful. Rather, David understood that he committed acts of sin because he was by birth a sinner (instead of being called a sinner because he had done evil deeds). In other words, the sinful nature preceded the sinful deeds.

Bible scholars have continued to debate the implications of original sin. In the medieval period, one reason babies were baptized was to remove the stain of original sin. Among Protestants, two differing views have emerged. On one hand is the perspective that God judges humans guilty not because of original sin but for their own acts of sin. Granted, all humans are born in sin, but God's grace has met this deficiency in everyone, and persons are condemned only for their own evil acts. On the other hand is the view that indeed God does consider each individual guilty before Him because he or she is "in Adam." Everyone who has been born—except for Jesus, who had no human father—is therefore under divine displeasure, not only because of their own acts of sin, but because "by nature we were children under wrath" (Eph 2:3).

REFLECTION: Why does modern society have so much trouble talking about sin? Do you think humans are born good or born sinful? What do you base your opinion on?

PRAYER: Holy Father, I confess that sin has tainted and haunted me all my life. Thank You that there is now life in Christ, even though there was death in Adam. Thank You that by Your grace, You call the vilest of sinners to forgiveness and new life in Christ. Amen.

22. Depravity

All of us have become like something unclean, and all our righteous acts are like a polluted garment; all of us wither like a leaf, and our iniquities carry us away like the wind.   Isaiah 64:6

DEFINITION: Depravity means tendency toward evil. Everyone is naturally inclined away from loving God and toward self-centeredness. Humans are not as sinful as they can possibly be, but they are tainted by evil through and through.

No parent ever had to teach a child to misbehave. When we stop and think about it seriously, doing the wrong thing comes naturally to all the sons and daughters of Adam and Eve. All are born enslaved to sin. Paul used this language in Romans 6:17: "You used to be slaves of sin." And "you offered the parts of yourselves as slaves to moral impurity, and to greater and greater lawlessness" (Rm 6:19). In Romans 7, he poignantly described the difficulty of indwelling sin: "I know that nothing good lives in me, that is, in my flesh" (Rm 7:18).

The biblical teaching on depravity is widely misunderstood. Scripture does not teach that all persons are as wicked as they can possibly be. Some are more deliberate in their acts of evil than others. Rather, depravity means that every part of the human person has been spoiled by sin. Our thinking processes have been distorted, our emotions are twisted, and we sometimes choose evil when we could choose good: "I do not do the good that I want to do, but I practice the evil that I do not want to do" (Rm 7:19).

Don't some people want to do good? Hasn't mankind achieved many positive things? Of course. Many acts of kindness and love are done by sinful human beings. Yet such deeds are based on mixed motives; they are not carried out supremely because of love for God and others. They fail to be complete because they "fall short of the glory of God"

(Rm 3:23). Apart from God's grace, all religion and altruism originate at best from the human imagination and impure affections and at worst from the Devil. This depravity was recognized as the cause for God's sending the flood: "When the LORD saw that man's wickedness was widespread on the earth and that every scheme his mind thought of was nothing but evil all the time, the Lord regretted that He had made man on the earth" (Gn 6:5-6).

Jeremiah noted how hard it is to be aware of one's own interior motives: "The heart is more deceitful than anything else and desperately sick—who can understand it?" (Jr 17:9). The greatest of saints have confessed the struggle against depravity throughout their lives. The depth of sin and the inability of humans to change on their own means that salvation is possible only because of God's loving grace rather than by any human merit or work. This teaching was summarized by the Latin phrase *sola gratia* (grace alone). This "theology of sin" was developed especially well in the Reformation era by those who found it in the writings of Augustine and Paul. This teaching is not to be confused with cynicism or fatalism. Rather we should be optimistic about God's love for His creation and His power to accomplish the good He intends. He even uses unbelieving sinners as His agents for His glory and for the good of the saints.

REFLECTION: Why does the biblical teaching on "depravity" seem so out of sync with modern society? How do you explain the relationship between depravity and *sola gratia*?

PRAYER: *Holy Lord, I know that my heart is so treacherous that I can't truly understand it. Show me my heart and give me the will and power to change. I need Your grace so that I will love You truly and rejoice in obeying Your word. Amen.*

23. The Devil

Be sober! Be on the alert! Your adversary the Devil is prowling around like a roaring lion, looking for anyone he can devour. Resist him, firm in the faith, knowing that the same sufferings are being experienced by your brothers in the world.   *1 Peter 5:8-9*

DEFINITION: **The Devil is a supernatural spirit creature hostile to God. He leads a host of other spirit beings in opposing God by tempting, accusing, leading astray, and other means. He is not equal to God and does not threaten God's sovereignty or power.**

The popular image of the Devil as a horned, fork-tailed, red-clad grinning imp ruling from hell owes nothing to Scripture and everything to fiction. The Devil (meaning "accuser") existed as an evil spirit before mankind was created, and Genesis 3:1-5 presents him as the serpent tempter (Rv 12:9). While it is possible that Isaiah 14 refers to his origin, what is certain is that he was created righteous and holy by God but fell into the sin of pride (1 Tm 3:6). He led other spirit beings into revolt against God, and God has been pleased to allow this opposition because it serves His glory and His purposes.

Human beings make two kinds of mistakes when thinking about the Devil. Some credit him with too much ability. As a creature he is finite in all ways, including knowledge and power. Others make too little of him, supposing that "Devil" is just a biblical way of referring to the impersonal effect of evil. ("The Devil made me do it" is a line that illustrates such a trivializing of the Enemy.) The most powerful twentieth-century treatment of the Devil was no doubt C. S. Lewis's brilliant parody, *The Screwtape Letters.*

In the Old Testament, the term "Satan" (meaning "adversary") is used to refer to this powerful wicked spirit. The most extensive passage is Job 1–2, in which he opposed Job before God and was permitted to attack Job within limits. In Genesis 3 and 1 Chronicles 21, Satan is a tempter urging humans to disobey God's word. By New Testament times, the doctrine of the Devil was more fully developed. Among other things, he is called the following:

Tempter (Mt 4:3)	Beelzebul (Mk 3:22)
Ruler of the demons (Lk 11:15)	Father of liars (Jn 8:44)
Ruler of this world (Jn 16:11)	God of this age (2 Co 4:4)
Angel of light (2 Co 11:14)	Ruler of the atmospheric domain (Eph 2:2)
The evil one (1 Jn 5:19)	Dragon (Rv 13:2)

In the Epistles the death and resurrection of Jesus are revealed as the means by which the Devil and his forces have been dealt a decisive blow (Col 1:15). Although the Devil has been defeated, he still tempts and is the adversary of believers, as the opening citation from 1 Peter 5:8-9 shows. Yet all believers can prevail against the Devil's tactics through the spiritual armor God has supplied (Eph 6:10-20). Revelation prophesies the utter demise of Satan: "The Devil who deceived them was thrown into the lake of fire and sulfur ... tormented day and night forever and ever" (Rv 20:10).

REFLECTION: Are you more prone to give the Devil too much credit or too little? Why? What difference does it make whether Christians believe in a literal, personal Devil?

PRAYER: Holy Creator, I praise You that Your plans cannot be thwarted by the wickedness of the Devil. Help me this day to take the full armor of God so that I may stand against the Devil's schemes, not in my strength but in the strength of Christ my Lord. Amen.

24. Demons

"If I drive out demons by Beelzebul, who is it your sons drive them out by? For this reason they will be your judges. If I drive out demons by the finger of God, then the kingdom of God has come to you."   *Luke 11:19-20*

DEFINITION: A demon is any of the wicked spirit creatures, without physical bodies, opposed to God. They are also called unclean spirits, evil spirits, and angels who sinned (therefore, fallen angels). There is only one Devil, but there are multitudes of demons.

Old Testament information about demons is sketchy, with King Saul's affliction being the most extensive example (1 Kg 16:14-23). Their origins are not discussed, but they were certainly created by God. Many evil spirits are permitted by God to do their dirty work among human beings. Yet some are so wicked, due to unnamed abominations, that God has permanently imprisoned them until their final demise (2 Pt 2:4). Additionally, some evil spirits appear to be condemned temporarily to "the abyss" (Lk 8:31; Rv 9:1-11). Their ultimate end will be eternal fire, the final destination of Satan, demons, and unregenerate humanity (Mt 25:41).

The most extensive information about demons in Scripture occurs in the Gospels. Jesus frequently encountered individuals in bondage to demons, and one hallmark of His ministry was His authority to drive out evil spirits on command (exorcism). He always prevailed over demons, one of the evidences that the kingdom of God had arrived. His death and resurrection guaranteed final doom for demons, just as it did for the Devil. The Book of Acts shows that the apostles continued to exorcise demons as evidence that they were clothed with Jesus' power. Throughout the centuries exorcism has been a more or less regular Christian practice. Demons have no physical bodies and are therefore invisible to humans, but they possess knowledge (Mk 1:24) and the ability to make certain choices (Mk 5:6-10). The descriptions of demons in Revelation note locust-like creatures and then later frog-like spirits (Rv 9:1-12; 16:13-16). According to the Epistles, evil spirits seek to corrupt sound doctrine, especially that Jesus is God's Son in the flesh (1 Tm 4:1-5; 1 Jn 4:1-3).

The work of demons has been observable in two ways especially. First is demon activity in psychic mediums that claim to communicate with the dead or to tell the future (1 Sm 28:1-25; Ac 16:16). Second is the demonic presence behind idolatry. Paul wrote that when pagans make sacrifices, "they sacrifice to demons" (1 Co 10:20). The biblical warnings against idolatry and consulting mediums are therefore serious indeed.

Humans possessed by demons exhibit symptoms such as great strength, behavioral abnormalities, and physical defects (Lk 8:26-30; 13:11-17). Demons are "junior" tempters under the Devil, and as such they urge humans into idolatry, immorality, and other violations of God's commands (Rv 9:20-21). Believers are the dwelling place of God's Spirit, so they cannot be "demonized" in the same way as others, yet many a Christian has endured demonic onslaught. The remedy is to use the spiritual armor God has provided (Eph 6:10-20) and to be led by the Spirit (Rm 8:12-17).

REFLECTION: How much do you agree that demons lie behind psychic phenomena and idolatry? Why? Have you ever thought you were being bothered by a demon? What did you do?

PRAYER: Lord Jesus, I acknowledge Your power over all the evil spirits. Help me to focus on Your power and not the power of the enemy—or my own impotence in the face of evil. Amen.

25.Antichrist

Children, it is the last hour. And as you have heard, "Antichrist is coming," even now many antichrists have come. We know from this that it is the last hour.   *1 John 2:18*

DEFINITION: The Greek *antichristos* means "against Christ" or "instead of Christ," and therefore refers to an enemy of Christ or one who attempts to usurp His position. Although the term is found only in John's epistles, the concept is found in a number of passages.

Surprisingly, the term "antichrist" appears only five times in four New Testament verses: 1 John 2:18,22; 4:3; 2 John 7. Whoever the antichrist turns out to be, these passages emphasize the *spirit* of antichrist already in the world. The Apostle John wanted Christians of his day to be on guard against that kind of antichrist. Likewise, today's believers are to be more diligent about identifying those trying to lead them astray from Jesus Christ than about trying to figure out who the final antichrist might be.

The Old Testament contains several passages about a potent end-time evil person or power that will attack God's people and that will be crushed eventually. Ezekiel 38–39 (the defeat of Gog) and Zechariah 12–14 are often cited. Much of what Daniel prophesied along these lines was fulfilled during the time of the Maccabean Revolt of the Jews (second century BC). Yet some of Daniel's visions find parallels in the New Testament and are therefore still in the future. Examples include these:

Daniel 11:36-37 ⟶ parallel to ⟶ 2 Thessalonians 2:4-6
Daniel 7:8,20-21; 8:24 ⟶ parallel to ⟶ Revelation 13:1-10

Jesus warned against false Christs and false prophets who try to lead astray His elect (Mt 24:24; Mk 13:22). He also mentioned "the abomination that causes desolation" spoken of by Daniel (Mt 24:15;

see Dn 9:27; 11:31; 12:11). In history, two events have already fulfilled the conditions for such a horror. First is the desecration of the Jewish temple by the Greek forces of Antiochus (around 168 BC); second is the destruction of the Jerusalem temple by the Romans under Titus (AD 70). Some—but by no means all—Bible students believe that there will be a similar future event caused by the forces of the final antichristian power. The most explicit teaching in Paul's letters is his description of a coming "man of lawlessness" (2 Th 2:3) who will claim to be God. John's language suggests that believers of his day expected a last-days antichrist of some sort (1 Jn 2:18).

The monstrous beast coming out the sea in Revelation 13:1-10 is similar to the horned beast of Daniel 7–8. He wars against God's people and is finally destroyed at the glorious coming of Christ (Rv 19). Whether this figure is a single individual or a symbolic representation of political power organized against God or something else has generated much debate. Frankly, no one can know for sure until it happens. Whatever happens, God will be victorious through the Lord Jesus. Our responsibility is to stand firm against today's antichrists (such as leaders of cults or pop cultural figures who mock Christ by their lifestyles). Our faith in Jesus the true Christ will enable us to overcome them.

REFLECTION: What sources of information should people turn to for information about antichrist? Why is it more important to be concerned about present antichrists than the future antichrist?

PRAYER: Lord Christ, keep me safe from deception by the spirit of antichrist already present. May I always be loyal to You, my Savior, the Son of God who came in the flesh. Amen.

26. Hell

"My friends, don't fear those who kill the body, and after that can do nothing more. But I will show you the One to fear: Fear Him who has the authority to throw people into hell after death. Yes, I say to you, this is the One to fear."

Luke 12:4-5

DEFINITION: Hell is the final place and condition of unregenerate humans (and evil spirits) in which they consciously suffer everlasting punishment, separated from God forever. It is a place of spiritual, psychological, and bodily torment from which there will never be hope of release.

"Hell" in the Bible is different than "the grave" (Hebrew *sheol*; Greek *hades*). In some passages *sheol-hades* means "the place where all the dead go, whether a place of happiness or punishment" (see Jb 3:13-22; Lk 10:15). In other texts, however, *sheol-hades* implies an intermediate place of punishment before the final judgment (Ps 49:14; Lk 16:23). The rest of this study focuses on hell as the ultimate doom of the wicked and notes other terms that deal with eternal punishment. Two notions predominate the biblical teaching: separation from God and condemnation (Jn 3:36; Mt 25:31-46).

Jesus had more to say about hell (Greek *gehenna*) than anyone else. In fact 11 of the 12 New Testament instances of *gehenna* are found on His lips. Thus, those who deny the reality of hell are basically accusing Him of falsehood. Further, the argument that God cannot justly punish someone *forever* for sins committed *in time* does not adequately consider that temporal sins insult the infinite holiness of God. If there is no hell, the holy God revealed in the Bible unjustly allows affronts to His righteous majesty to go unpunished.

How long does hell last? The term in the New Testament is "eternal" (Greek *aionios*), from the noun "eon" or "age" (Greek *aion*). For the biblical writers there were two ages: this age and the age to come (Mk

10:30; Eph 1:21). "This age" was temporary; the coming age was everlasting. As surely as the eternal life of the redeemed will be endless in heaven, so the punishment of the damned will be endless in hell. With reference to the future condition of the wicked, *aionios* plainly means endless duration (Mt 18:8; 2 Th 1:9; Hb 6:2).

What is the nature of hell's torment? Without doubt the Scriptures teach that hell is a literal place and a permanent condition. Some of the phrases used are these:

Outer darkness (Mt 8:12)	Eternal fire prepared for the Devil (Mt 25:41)
Their worm does not die (Mk 9:48)	Wrath [of God] (1 Th 2:16)
Everlasting destruction (2 Th 1:9)	Lake of fire (Rv 20:15)
Second death (Rv 21:8)	Outside [the holy city] (Rv 22:15)

It is hard to understand how these can be all simultaneously true if they are all equally literal. (How can we conceptualize complete darkness in a fiery lake?) Thus, some believe that these descriptions are figurative of something indescribably horrible, just as the description of heaven as a massive, cube-like city in Revelation 21 symbolizes something indescribably wonderful. Throughout the centuries, however, most Christian thinkers have believed that the description of fire so dominates the biblical account of hell that it must entail literal flames.

REFLECTION: Why is it important to believe that hell is a literal place? How would you counsel someone who said, "Hell is just the bad stuff you go through on earth"?

PRAYER: *Lord Jesus, help me to see others around me as destined for hell unless they come to You in faith. May I testify this day to the reality of my belief in heaven and hell. Amen.*

V. JESUS

National magazines still put Jesus on their covers, often around Christmas and Easter. Television networks feature popular specials on the search for the real Jesus. A movie star releases a film about the suffering and death of Jesus that attracts millions of viewers and becomes one of the greatest money-making movies of all time. Clearly Jesus is still a person of interest for our increasingly secularized culture.

Which Jesus shall we follow? Several versions of Jesus are out there. For some, He was a humble Jewish rabbi whose gentle teachings were hijacked by people like Paul and turned into a Savior that He never meant to be. He's been called a magician as well as a great psychologist. In the twentieth century, persons perceiving themselves to be powerless and trampled on by majority culture championed Him as the great Liberator. A feminist Christ, a Latin American Christ, and a Christ for homosexuals are among several that emerged. In traditional forms of Christianity, He's an object of mystical devotion. Crucifixes and sacramental ceremonies aid such Christ-mystics, some of whom report visions of Him.

How does all this square with the Jesus of the four Gospels? How did Christians of the early centuries come to understand Him? They were deeply concerned to get this right. The longest sections in both the Apostles' Creed and the Nicene Creed describe His person and work. The classic understanding of Jesus has consistently identified with these confessions. As we will see in the following seven studies, such truths were already clearly laid out in the Scriptures.

27. Son of God

Jesus performed many other signs in the presence of His disciples that are not written in this book. But these are written so that you may believe Jesus is the Messiah, the Son of God, and by believing you may have life in His name.   John 20:30-31

DEFINITION: "Son of God" means more than that Jesus was divine or a special messenger sent from God to the world. "Son of God" means that Jesus is fully God Himself, equal in power and glory to God the Father and God the Spirit.

During the earliest centuries, biblical scholars debated the interpretation of the New Testament statements about Jesus. How could Jesus the human being also be God's Son? Many opposing views brought great Christian minds together to discuss this. These issues were mainly resolved at the Council of Nicea (AD 325) and the Council of Chalcedon (AD 451).

Two special terms have been used by Christian thinkers to describe the identity of Jesus in relationship to God. First is "hypostatic union." This means that, after He was born of Mary, Jesus Christ has been one Person but with two natures: humanity and deity. These natures are mysteriously united so that the humanity is not lost in the deity nor the deity lost in the humanity. The two natures are not mixed together but each retains its own character.

The second term is "Trinity." (See the article on the Trinity.) This includes belief that Jesus alone, the Son of God, is God the Son. The three Persons of the Godhead are one God. This belief has been rejected by sects that consider Jesus to be the divine Savior but less than fully God. The orthodox Christian confessions condemned such views, insisting that He has been eternally begotten of the Father, begotten, not created.

Most Christians are content simply to affirm that Jesus is both fully God and fully human without following the technical debates. Yet we should be grateful for those who were concerned to use precise language to spell out this central matter of Christian faith. Following are the most important biblical phrases that served as essential data for Christian beliefs about the hypostatic union and the Trinity.

- "Baptizing them in the name of the Father and of the Son and of the Holy Spirit" (Mt 28:19).
- "The beginning of the gospel of Jesus Christ, the Son of God" (Mk 1:1).
- "The angel replied to her: ... 'The holy One to be born will be called the Son of God'" (Lk 1:35).
- "In the beginning was the Word, and the Word was with God, and the Word was God" (Jn 1:1).
- "The Word became flesh and took up residence among us" (Jn 1:14).
- "Established as the powerful Son of God by the resurrection from the dead" (Rm 1:4).
- "From them by physical descent, came the Messiah, who is God over all" (Rm 9:5).
- "For God was pleased to have all His fullness dwell in Him [Christ]" (Col 1:19).
- "For in Him the entire fullness of God's nature dwells bodily" (Col 2:9).
- "We wait for the blessed hope and ... our great God and Savior, Jesus Christ" (Ti 2:13).
- "[Christ] is the radiance of His [God's] glory, the exact expression of His nature" (Hb 1:3).

REFLECTION: Why do some people make a distinction between Jesus as "Son of God" and as "God the Son"? How important was it for Christians to insist that these mean the same thing?

PRAYER: *Holy Lord Jesus, I confess with the Christians of old that You are the unique "Son of God, eternally begotten of the Father, God from God, Light from Light, true God from true God, begotten, not made, of one Being with the Father." Amen (citation from the Nicene Creed).*

28. Virgin Birth

"See, the virgin will become pregnant and give birth to a son, and they will name Him Immanuel," which is translated "God is with us." When Joseph got up from sleeping, he ... married her [Mary] but did not know her intimately until she gave birth to a son.

Matthew 1:23-25

DEFINITION: Mary, the mother of Jesus, was sexually chaste both when she conceived Him and when He was born. The Holy Spirit "overshadowed" Mary, bringing about her pregnancy.

The biblical teaching about Mary's sexual status when Jesus was conceived and born is in Matthew 1 and Luke 1. Matthew regarded the prophecy of Isaiah 7:14 about the virgin becoming pregnant as fulfilled in Jesus' birth. The language used by the Gospel writers is both explicit and discreet. Mary's status is certain from the word "virgin" (Greek *parthenos*). Its only possible meaning in Greek was a sexually inexperienced, unmarried woman. To this may be added Mary's questioning of the angel: "How can this be, since I have not been intimate with a man?" (Lk 1:34). Further, one should consider Joseph's skepticism about Mary's pregnancy, which was overcome only by angelic revelation (Mt 1:18-21). The ancients were not as sophisticated in their understanding of human reproduction as we are today, but it would be foolish to suppose that they did not grasp the connection between sexual intimacy and a baby's conception. (Note: the phrase "immaculate conception," believed by some, refers not to Jesus' conception in Mary's womb but to Mary's conception in her mother's womb.)

Those whose view of the universe excludes miracles of course have difficulty with the Gospels at many points. But if every miracle is removed from them, an entirely different Jesus emerges. He is reduced, at best, to a great moral teacher with keen insight. Further, if the Gospel writers got the beginning of the story wrong, the rest of their account of Jesus is also suspect.

Many Christians have pondered why the New Testament virgin birth material is so limited. Why are there no references to it in the Epistles if the virgin birth was known from the beginning? First, this teaching more appropriately belongs to Christian instruction than to basic evangelism. (Conversion does not come by believing in the virgin birth.) The gospel message focuses on Christ's death and deity; the virgin birth is part of Christian education. Second, the Epistles were written mainly to address specific problems. Their silence on the virgin birth is evidence that early churches never had a problem accepting this teaching.

This is confirmed by the fact that all the early Christian confessions included "born of the Virgin Mary" or parallel statements. No early debates on this surfaced (in contrast, for example, to the Trinity). The virgin birth answers the question, "How did God become man?" Throughout the centuries, three Christian teachings have been bound together closely. In most cases, someone who has denied any one of these has ultimately concluded that none of them is true:

- *Deity:* Jesus is fully the Son of God; therefore, He is Lord and God.
- *Incarnation:* God the one and only Son (the second Person of the Trinity) became human.
- *Virgin birth:* Jesus was conceived and born to the Virgin Mary.

REFLECTION: Why do the deity, incarnation, and virgin birth doctrines stand or fall together? How much do you agree that teaching the virgin birth belongs to discipleship rather than evangelism?

PRAYER: *Lord Christ, You humbled Yourself to enter the virgin's womb, taking on human flesh. I confess that You are God incarnate, the Son of God, one with the Father. Yet You ever live as a resurrected and glorified human, whose resurrection likeness I will someday share. Amen.*

29. Messiah

*The Spirit of the Lord G*od *is on Me, because the L*ord *has anointed Me to bring good news to the poor. He has sent Me to heal the brokenhearted, to proclaim liberty to the captives, and freedom to the prisoners; to proclaim the year of the L*ord*'s favor.*   Isaiah 61:1-2

DEFINITION: **"Messiah" is the English spelling of a Hebrew (Old Testament) term meaning "anointed one." This title referred to the One promised by the prophets. In Greek (New Testament), the same term is "Christ." Early Christians turned "Christ" into a name for Jesus.**

The biggest difference between present-day followers of Jesus and current practitioners of Judaism is whether the Messiah promised in the Hebrew Scriptures came historically in the person of Jesus. Judaism answers the question no; Christians—as the very name implies—answer the question yes.

Without doubt the Hebrew prophets predicted a special work of God in reinstating His people to full fellowship with Himself. This would happen through the dynasty of the house of David that would last forever (2 Sm 7:14). Isaiah understood this in terms of a coming Prince of Peace who would rule from David's throne without end (9:6-7; see Lk 1:32-33).

None of the four Gospels makes sense apart from the conviction that Jesus fulfilled the prophecies about a coming Messiah. Matthew cited several predictions that Jesus fulfilled (for example, 1:22-23; 4:14-15; 12:17-18; 27:9-10). Mark opened his Gospel by identifying Jesus as Christ. According to Luke, Jesus quoted Isaiah 61:1-2, cited above, and claimed that He fulfilled it in His own person (4:17-21). John's Gospel shows that both Jews and others recognized Jesus as the Messiah. Indeed, the Fourth Gospel was written to show that Jesus is the promised Messiah who gives eternal life to all who believe in Him (1:41-42; 4:25-26; 20:30-31).

"Christ" quickly became a standard way for believers to refer to Jesus, and the word is found more than 400 times in the Epistles. Of these, more than 200 have simply "Christ" as His name, while more than 100 instances have "Jesus Christ" and more than 80 have "Christ Jesus." Of these, more than 50 have the fuller "Lord Jesus Christ," and most striking of all is the complete name "our Lord Jesus Christ" (or "Jesus Christ our Lord"), occurring more than 30 times. By contrast, there is no instance of "my Christ," as if to emphasize that He is Lord over an entire community of those believing in and loyal to Him.

In the Old Testament, two kinds of Israelite leaders were literally anointed with oil as a symbol of their official status: priests and kings (Ex 28:41; 1 Sm 16:12). This provides important clues about how the first Christians understood Jesus as the Anointed One. According to the Book of Hebrews, Jesus is a priest who offered Himself on behalf of His people and intercedes for them (7:25; 9:11-12). According to Revelation, Jesus is King of kings and will rule His redeemed people forever (17:14).

REFLECTION: How does it help your relationship to Jesus to know that He fulfilled prophecies? What difference does it make that priests and kings in the Old Testament were anointed ones?

PRAYER: *Dear Lord Jesus Christ, thank You for coming in fulfillment of the biblical prophecies about the coming Messiah. Thank You that as High Priest, you gave Yourself as a perfect sacrifice for sin. Thank You that as King of kings, You rule over all Your people today and that You will come again as King of kings. Amen.*

30. Kingdom of God

Jesus went to Galilee, preaching the good news of God: "The time is fulfilled, and the kingdom of God has come near. Repent and believe in the good news."   Mark 1:14-15

DEFINITION: The kingdom of God is His rule through His messianic King. According to Jesus' teaching, the kingdom was both present and future. All who believe in and follow Him are already in the kingdom, yet the kingdom will be gloriously revealed at the return of Christ.

Aside from teaching about the meaning of His coming death, no topic was more important to Jesus than the kingdom of God. This phrase or the equivalent "kingdom of heaven" occurs about 80 times in the Gospels. The usual English translation is not particularly good, for the kingdom (Greek *basileia*) is not a place but rather a condition or state of affairs. John the Baptist had announced that the kingdom was near, meaning that the promised Messiah was about to arrive. Later, Jesus proclaimed that it had already arrived (Mt 12:28). He brought the kingdom because He was the King of the kingdom. It arrived in His person.

Jesus proclaimed the kingdom in a way that diverged sharply from the typical first-century Jewish expectation. The Jews were generally looking for a military-political leader who would destroy the Roman yoke. His coming (the Day of the Lord) would be sudden, irresistible, and visible to everyone. The Jewish understanding looked something like this:

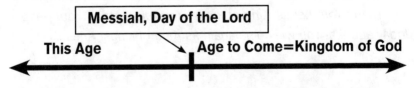

Jesus' view was shaped by His understanding that, as the Messiah, He was to have two comings, not just one. Thus, in His first coming,

He truly brought the kingdom. Yet He brought it in a form that was gradual, resistible, and largely invisible. Only in His second coming in glory will the kingdom come with irresistible might. His understanding was like this:

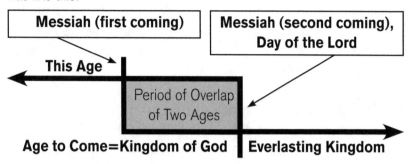

Jesus' first coming brought the age to come. Yet He did not do away with this age, which will occur only at His return. Thus, followers of Jesus today experience the tension of being partakers of the kingdom—submitting to the King as Lord and Savior—yet still living in this rebellious age. Jesus explained that His followers are in the world but not of the world (Jn 17:13-14). Thus, Jesus inaugurated the kingdom of God in His first coming, but in His second coming He will consummate the kingdom.

REFLECTION: Why should today's followers of Christ consider the kingdom to be important? Describe the differences between this age and the age to come (the kingdom of God).

PRAYER: Father, I praise You that Your Son reigns as King over the kingdom. I want to live joyfully today as His loyal subject. I long for the day when the kingdom will be complete. Amen.

31. Son of Man

I saw One like a son of man coming with the clouds of heaven. He approached the Ancient of Days and was escorted before Him. He was given authority to rule, and glory, and a kingdom.... His kingdom is one that will not be destroyed.   Daniel 7:13-14

DEFINITION: A phrase occurring in both Testaments, "Son of Man" was Jesus' favorite title for Himself. In the Old Testament it usually meant "human being," but in Daniel 7 He was a mysterious messianic figure. Jesus used this title as an alternative to calling Himself the Messiah.

In Hebrew, "son of man" (*ben adam*) meant an individual member of the species "mankind." (*Adam* means "man.") The LORD called Ezekiel "son of man" many times, emphasizing his mere humanity. The Israelite king was likewise the "son of man" whom God made strong for Himself (Ps 80:17). Daniel 7:13-14 is different, for no mere human could be so magnificent. Jesus understood this "son of man" to be a prophecy about Himself as Messiah. He alluded to Daniel's Son of Man coming in a cloud with power and glory in His Olivet Discourse about His return (Mt 24:30). He also quoted Daniel 7:13 at His trial (Mt 26:64) to answer the high priest about whether He was the Messiah. Long ago the great preacher Augustine wrote, "The Son of God became the Son of Man so that the sons of men might be made sons of God."

The Gospels contain more than 80 instances in which Jesus used "Son of Man" to refer to Himself. In doing so, He was proclaiming that He fulfilled Daniel 7. Neither His enemies nor His disciples, however, seemed to grasp what He was doing. Thus, no one in the Gospels ever addressed Him by that title even though He rarely called Himself anything else. Evidently the term "Christ" was preferred by the early believers. The only New Testament passages in which "Son of Man" appears outside the Gospels are Acts 7:56 and Revelation 1:13; 14:14.

Sometimes Jesus used "Son of Man" as a simple substitute for the pronoun "I" (Mt 11:19; Lk 9:58). "Son of Man" sayings, however, occur in a number of places in which Jesus was emphasizing particular aspects of His identity as the Messiah:

- He who would suffer and die (Mk 9:12,31; 10:33; 14:21,41)
- He who would give His life as a ransom for many (Mt 20:28)
- He who would be raised from the dead (Mt 17:9)
- He who will return to earth in great splendor (Lk 17:24; 18:8)
- He who can forgive sins and interpret the law (Lk 5:16; 6:5; 19:20)
- He who will judge mankind (Mt 13:41; 25:31-32)

Two passages show with great clarity that Jesus used "Son of Man" to refer to His true humanity, His messiahship, and His deity all at once. The first is in His encounter with Nicodemus, in which His heavenly origin, His being lifted up, and His being the object of faith for eternal life are affirmed (Jn 3:13-14). The second is Peter's confession about who the Son of Man is: "You are the Messiah, the Son of the living God" (Mt 16:16).

REFLECTION: How important is it to understand that for Jesus "Son of Man" meant more than "human being"? Why do you suppose the Epistles never used "Son of Man" as a title for Jesus?

PRAYER: Lord Jesus, You are the heavenly Son of Man whom Daniel foresaw. Not only did You humble Yourself and become man, You knew Yourself to be the Messiah, the Lord from heaven. Thank You for coming as the Son of Man to seek and save what was lost. Amen.

32. Atonement

How much more will the blood of the Messiah, who through the eternal Spirit offered Himself without blemish to God, cleanse our consciences from dead works to serve the living God?

Hebrews 9:14

DEFINITION: Atonement refers to reconciling alienated parties by making amends, that is, by fully satisfying the penalty so that the offense is removed and the relationship is restored. In Scripture, Christ's death provided atonement in that He died as a substitute for sinners.

What was the meaning of Christ's death? How did He view His mission of suffering and death? We know from the words He spoke at the first Lord's Supper that He understood the crucifixion as "for the forgiveness of sins." Explaining what this means has occupied the energies of many a theologian and minister. Some have taught that He died a moral example of righteous suffering, but surely it was much more than this.

Over the centuries, the best thinking has been done by those who understand the New Testament to be teaching a "substitutionary atonement." The precedent is found in the Old Testament system of sacrifices that required animal blood to be shed. The Lord told the Israelites through Moses that the animal's blood makes "atonement on the altar for your lives, since it is the lifeblood that makes atonement" (Lv 17:11). Yet as Hebrews 9:11-15 teaches, these sacrifices were mere shadows and types, looking ahead to the one sacrifice that would provide forgiveness.

The atonement is the biblical solution to two sets of truths that could not otherwise have been reconciled. On one hand is the holiness of God and His wrath against sin. He cannot look at sin and His justice requires that He must punish it (Jr 44:4; Rm 2:5-9). "The wages of sin is death" (Rm 6:23). On the other hand is the love and grace of God extended toward helpless, hopeless sinners. The resolution of this difficulty was for God Himself to provide the satisfaction for sin by sending His own sinless Son to pay the terrible price to satisfy His wrath. Thus when a sinner places faith in Jesus, God grants forgiveness and at the same time retains His own righteousness (Rm 3:26).

The Bible abounds with a variety of terms to refer to the meaning of Jesus' death.

- *Substitution*: the death of One on behalf of many (Mt 26:28; Rm 5:12-21)
- *Sacrifice*: the violent shedding of Jesus' blood as the Lamb of God (Jn 1:29; Rv 1:5)
- *Ransom*: paying the price to set us free from sin's slavery and penalty (Mt 20:28; Mk 10:45)
- *Redemption*: paying the price to gain release from the law's curse (Gl 3:13-14; 1 Pt 1:18)
- *Propitiation*: quenching God's wrath against sinners (Rm 3:25; 1 Jn 2:2)
- *Expiation*: removal of sin by being punished and paying the penalty (Ac 10:43; Col 2:13-14)

No better summary of the message of the atonement can be found than Paul's teaching in 2 Corinthians 5:21: "[God] made the One who did not know sin to be sin for us, so that we might become the righteousness of God in Him."

REFLECTION: Why was it important for Jesus to view His death as an atoning sacrifice? Explain "atonement" in your own words. Which term from the list do you prefer for Jesus' death? Why?

PRAYER: *Lamb of God, Your death paid the penalty for my rebellion against God and against His glory. Thanks be to God that in Your death there is atonement, a sacrifice of redemption in which the wrath of God was satisfied. Amen.*

33. Resurrection

[They] said, "The Lord has certainly been raised, and has appeared to Simon!" Then they began to describe what had happened on the road and how He was made known to them in the breaking of the bread.   Luke 24:34-35

DEFINITION: The resurrection of Jesus means His rising from the dead on the third day after His crucifixion, in bodily form, transformed so that His body can never die again. Evidence for His resurrection focuses on the empty tomb and the appearances of the living Christ.

Christianity stands or falls on the bodily resurrection of Jesus Christ. If God raised Him from the dead, then His claims to speak the truth and to be God's Son are vindicated: "[He] was established as the powerful Son of God by the resurrection from the dead" (Rm 1:4). If the resurrection did not happen, "Your faith is worthless; you are still in your sins.... We should be pitied more than anyone" (1 Co 15:17,19). This obviously goes far beyond believing that somehow the "Christ spirit" survived His death.

All four Gospels report that the tomb in which Jesus' body was buried and sealed was empty on Sunday. However several alternate theories have been offered: the women went to the wrong tomb; the disciples stole the body; He didn't really die but had been unconscious. Only His bodily resurrection can adequately explain the empty tomb. Gospels, Acts, Epistles, and Revelation alike report the appearances of the resurrected Jesus. The only way to "explain away" this evidence is by a theory of hallucination. It is easier to believe the resurrection as reported than to believe that so many different people hallucinated exactly the same thing under such a great variety of conditions. (See Josh McDowell's *Evidence That Demands a Verdict.*)

Jesus presented Himself alive five times on Easter Day: to women at the tomb (Mt 28:1-10); to Mary Magdalene (Jn 20:11-18); to Peter (Lk 24:34; 1 Co 15:5); to two travelers (Lk 24:13-32); and to ten apostles (Jn 20:19-25). Seven more appearances are reported: to eleven apostles in Jerusalem (Jn 20:26-31); to seven at the Sea of Galilee (Jn 21:1-3); to eleven apostles in Galilee (Mt 28:16-20); to more than 500 (1 Co 15:6); to His brother James (1 Co 15:7); at His ascension 40 days after the resurrection (Lk 24:44-49); and to Saul of Tarsus on the way to Damascus (1 Co 15:8).

The resurrection of Jesus was different in quality from other raisings reported in Scriptures. Lazarus, for example, had life returned to his body, but he was not transformed so that he could not die again. Thus, until the dead in Christ are raised, He alone has experienced true resurrection. He is therefore called "the firstfruits of those who have fallen asleep" (1 Co 15:20). What was Jesus' resurrection body like? The Gospels and Epistles alike yield little direct information. The longest discussion is found in 1 Corinthians 15:35-49, which says that "if there is a natural body, there is also a spiritual body" and "we will also bear the image of the heavenly man" (vv. 44,49). Those who have received salvation in Christ have already begun to experience "the power of His resurrection" (Php 3:10) and are therefore assured that they will be raised eternally at His coming.

REFLECTION: Do you believe Christianity stands or falls with the bodily resurrection of Jesus? Why or why not? What evidence for the resurrection do you find the most persuasive?

PRAYER: Risen Lord, You conquered death and are alive forever. I worship You this day as the One whom the grave could not hold. Thank You for securing my own coming resurrection. Amen.

VI.SALVATION

When the city jailer of Philippi was roused one midnight, he asked the prisoners Paul and Silas, "Sirs, what must I do to be saved?" (Ac 16:30). Every religion of the world provides a different answer to the jailer's question. The answer given that night is profound in its simplicity: "Believe on the Lord Jesus, and you will be saved—you and your household" (Ac. 16:31). Yet as simple as that answer appears on the surface, Christ's followers have understood it in a great variety of ways. What, after all, does it mean to "believe"? Perhaps the jailer wasn't even asking a question about saving his eternal soul; maybe he was more concerned about being rescued from the stress caused by the earthquake and the supposition that the prisoners had fled.

In any case, "salvation" is the broadest term used both in the Bible and by Christian teachers to discuss the sinner's rescue from death to life with God. Many indeed prefer to speak of "salvation in three tenses." God *has saved* the sinner in conversion; He *is saving* the sinner throughout this life; He *will save* the sinner at the resurrection.

The six words presented in this section focus on salvation in its beginning stages, that is, at conversion. Yet all of them at the same time include implications for things the "saved" person will experience from that moment and forward throughout eternity.

34. Gospel

Now brothers, I want to clarify for you the gospel I proclaimed to you; you received it and have taken your stand on it. You are also saved by it, if you hold to the message I proclaimed to you—unless you believed to no purpose.   *1 Corinthians 15:1-2*

DEFINITION: Gospel literally means "good news." "Gospel" refers in Scripture mainly to the message that through the life, death, and resurrection of Christ, God graciously acted to establish His kingdom and now welcomes into His family sinners who repent and receive Christ by faith.

In its original secular setting the gospel (Greek *euangelion,* good news) referred to a message about a military victory, the birth of a king, or some other momentous event. After the first century AD, "Gospel" came to refer to one of the books written about Jesus' life. (Only four Gospels were considered inspired, although other writings were called Gospels.) But in the New Testament, "gospel" refers to the Christian good news, not to a book.

Jesus' ministry after He was baptized was characterized by His proclaiming the gospel (Mt 4:23; Mk 1:14; Lk 4:43). This explicitly included the news about the kingdom. (See the article on the kingdom of God.) It is a matter of some curiosity that John's Gospel—which emphasizes faith in Jesus more than the others—does not directly use terms for "gospel."

After Christ's resurrection, the message proclaimed always included the good news about Jesus' death for sinners and His resurrection as living Lord. The Book of Acts is filled with many such examples (5:42; 8:12; 11:20; 20:24). Study of Acts suggests that gospel presentations normally included the following elements:

1. Jesus' historical ministry included miracles and teaching about God's kingdom.

2. He suffered and was crucified by wicked people, dying on the cross for sinners.
3. God raised Him from the dead, demonstrating that He is Messiah and God's Son.
4. He is the exalted Lord and Savior at God's right hand.
5. Sinners everywhere are invited to repent and turn to Jesus for forgiveness of sins.
6. Everyone who believes will receive God's Spirit and become part of God's family.

Paul was particularly concerned to preserve the true gospel and urged the Galatians to resist "a different gospel" (Gl 1:6). For this reason, Christians in the early centuries labored diligently to proclaim the right understanding of God and Christ in succinct forms, such as the Apostles' Creed and the Nicene Creed, which have received universal acceptance from Christians. During the sixteenth century, the nature of gospel salvation was clarified by the famous "five pillars of the Reformation" (salvation as taught in Scripture alone, by Christ alone, by grace alone, through faith alone, to the glory of God alone).

Those who embrace the gospel inevitably have their lives transformed so that they love and delight in God (2 Co 4:6). To believe the gospel marks the beginning of an eternity of knowing Christ (Php 3:7-10). Versions of the "gospel" that stress God's gifts and blessings more than receiving and enjoying God Himself are distorted at best and heretical at worst.

REFLECTION: What is the difference between the gospel and a Gospel? Why is it important for gospel presentations to include both proclamation of truth and invitation to respond?

PRAYER: *Lord Jesus, the good news is about You more than about me. I praise You that You are actively seeking to convert sinners into saints who will love and enjoy You forever. Help me remember that the gospel means receiving You more than getting Your blessings. Amen.*

35. Predestination

For those He foreknew He also predestined to be conformed to the image of His Son, so that He would be the firstborn among many brothers. And those He predestined, He also called; and those He called, He also justified; and those He justified, He also glorified.

Romans 8:29-30

DEFINITION: Predestination means that God has marked out ahead of time or predetermined certain things that shall come to pass. In particular, God has marked out certain persons for salvation or service. Such individuals are called in Scripture the elect or chosen.

This concept—troubling to many, a comfort for others—remains at the center of much debate among sincere Christians, particularly in reference to the idea that God predetermines some for salvation. On one hand, everyone who takes the Bible seriously "believes in" predestination in some way, for the texts cannot be avoided. In any event one of the best known designations of the Old Testament people of God (Israel) was "the chosen people." On the other hand, devout Bible students have sharply disagreed about the *basis* of predestination.

Some devout Christians believe that predestination is simply God's foreknowledge at work. Because God knows all things ahead of time, He knows who will respond freely in faith to the gospel. These are His elect. This perspective is often identified by the label Arminianism, and it emphasizes human free will. As an example, among English-speaking Christians, spiritual descendants of John Wesley (Methodist, holiness, and Pentecostal groups in particular) have been likely to understand predestination along these lines.

Others, equally devout, believe that human sin has so disabled everyone that none would ever believe in Christ unless God first chose them to be recipients of salvation. God graciously selected some (but not all) to become His children. Those whom He has chosen ultimately will respond to the gospel in faith. This point of view goes by the label Calvinism or Reformed theology, and it emphasizes God's sovereignty in salvation. Spiritual descendants of Martin Luther and John Calvin (Lutheran and Presbyterian groups, for example) emphasize this perspective. (Some early English-speaking Baptists were Arminian and some were Calvinist, and even today some Baptists espouse one view; some the other view; and still others are undecided.)

The verb translated "predestine" occurs in six New Testament verses: Acts 4:28; Romans 8:29-30; 1 Corinthians 2:7; Ephesians 1:5,11. What is striking in examining these passages is their emphasis on God's initiative predetermining to accomplish His purposes through Jesus Christ. Also, in the majority of instances, it is *persons* who are predestined.

The passages that use the language of predestination state its *source* as God's power and will (Ac. 4:28) or His pleasure and will (Eph 1:5,11). The *outcome* for those who have been predestined is conformity to Christ's image (Rm 8:29); their glory (Rm 8:30; 1 Co 2:7); and praise to God's glory (Eph 1:11-12). Remembering this objective would help make this topic less divisive. We should focus instead on God's grace in choosing persons for salvation.

REFLECTION: How much do you agree that "Everyone who takes the Bible seriously 'believes in' predestination"? To what extent have you been exposed to teaching on predestination?

PRAYER: Dear Father, Your Word teaches that You have chosen persons for salvation. Help me to focus on what I do understand about it rather than what I don't. Without Your help, I will never be conformed to Christ's image or reach final glory. I want to love You and Your ways so much that I bring praise to Your glory, now and forever. In Jesus' name, amen.

36. Regeneration

He saved us—not by works of righteousness that we had done, but according to His mercy, through the washing of regeneration and renewal by the Holy Spirit.   Titus 3:5

DEFINITION: Regeneration or being born again refers to God's act of making a person alive spiritually. This is the supernatural work of the Holy Spirit by which sinners are given new spiritual life enabling them to relate to God in faith, love, obedience, and delight.

The noun "regeneration" occurs twice only in the New Testament, Titus 3:5 and Matthew 19:28 (referring to creation). Yet the concept abounds. A closely related verb form is used in 1 Peter 1:23: "You have been born again … through the living and enduring word of God." The longest passage is John 3:1-8, Jesus' discourse with Nicodemus about being born again or born from above. Jesus made it plain that a person must experience this new birth in order to enter the kingdom of God. No one has been born again apart from the work of the Spirit. In other places in John's writings this is called being "born of God" (Jn 1:13; 1 Jn 3:9).

Paul's letters speak similarly. We have been "made alive" with Christ and are now "renewed" (Rm 12:2; Ti 3:5). The old life has gone; a new life has come (Rm 6:4). The effect of regeneration is to change the human heart from spiritual death to spiritual life, so that there is now a new creation (2 Co 5:17). This change was foreseen in several Old Testament passages, notably the New Covenant prophecy of Jeremiah 31:31-34 (see also Dt 30:6).

Some theologians, notably those in the Roman Catholic tradition, have interpreted the Bible to mean that regeneration occurs at the time of (and because of) water baptism. This rises from a misunderstanding of Jesus' words about the need to be "born of water and the

Spirit" (Jn 3:5). He was referring to the cleansing action of the word of God along the lines prophesied in Ezekiel 36:24-27 and noted in 1 Peter 1:23, cited above. The biblical understanding sees baptism as a testimony that regeneration has already occurred, rather than as a means to receive it. Regeneration is the sovereign task of the Holy Spirit (1 Co 2:6-16).

Regeneration happens at the moment of conversion. Yet the logical relationship between the Spirit's regenerating work in a sinner and that sinner's repentance and faith has been the focus of much heated discussion. Is faith the *basis* upon which the Spirit regenerates or is faith the *fruit* of regeneration? The biblical language, emphasizing regeneration as moving from death to life and as sovereignly worked by the Spirit, appears to favor the latter view and understands faith itself as a gift from God. One illustration sometimes used is that human infants breathe because they have been born, not in order to be born. The life of the infant came as a result of the act of the human father. Similarly Christians "breathe spiritually" (exhaling = repentance; inhaling = faith) because they have already received life from their heavenly Father (1 Jn 4:7).

Although many Christians remember the exact circumstances in which they were born again, others are uncertain. Our responsibility is to know whether we have received spiritual life (evidenced by "spiritual breathing"), not the time and place we were regenerated.

REFLECTION: How important is it to emphasize that being born again is the sovereign responsibility of the Spirit? How certain are you that you have experienced regeneration?

PRAYER: *Holy Spirit, Yours is the work of giving new life to those once dead in trespasses and sin. Only life from You could enable me to love God and to live in happy obedience to Him as my Father. Let my life today reflect that I am a new creation in Christ. Amen.*

37. Justification

Therefore, let it be known to you, brothers, that through this man [Jesus] forgiveness of sins is being proclaimed to you, and everyone who believes in Him is justified from everything, which you could not be justified from through the law of Moses.   Acts 13:38-39

DEFINITION: Justification is God's judicial declaration that a sinner who believes in Christ is counted righteous instead of guilty, based on Jesus' death on his or her behalf. Christ's righteousness is imputed (reckoned) to the sinner just as God imputed sin to Christ on the cross.

The language of justification is primarily legal or forensic, based on the biblical notion, "Won't the Judge of all the earth do what is just?" (Gn 18:25). The following facts provide the background for understanding the biblical teaching on justification.

- God always does (and pronounces judgment) according to what is righteous.
- All mankind must appear before Him for judgment.
- All persons are guilty of sin before Him.

If there is any hope for a human to be acquitted—to escape God's condemnation—then God must justify those who are in fact guilty before Him. And the way He does this with integrity is by a kind of bookkeeping exchange: God credits Christ's righteous life and sacrificial death to sinners, so that sinners do not bear the penalty of their sins; rather Christ has already done so. In the words of Paul, God "declares righteous the ungodly" through faith (Rm 4:5).

Paul is the biblical writer who fully developed justification as the foundation for understanding salvation. (Of the 39 instances of the verb "justify" in the New Testament, 29 of them come from Paul's letters or recorded words.) He found the key for this in Genesis 15:6: "Abram believed the LORD, and He credited it to him as righteousness" (see Rm 4:3,9,22; Gl 3:16). Martin Luther in the sixteenth century made his rediscovery of "justification by faith alone" the touchstone of the Reformation. This differed from justification by faith plus good works or keeping of the law, and this has been the distinguishing mark of Protestants ever since.

Careful Bible students have maintained these distinct ways to speak of justification:

- Justification by God's grace: God's undeserved favor is the origin or source of righteousness.
- Justification by Christ's blood: Jesus' death is the ground or basis of one's righteousness.
- Justification by faith: the sinner's trust is the instrument or condition of righteousness. In particular, this means that faith is itself never to be considered a good work that is somehow the sinner's contribution to salvation. (See the article on faith.)

To this should be added the discussion from the Epistle of James that good works are the expected *fruit* or *evidence* that one has been justified (Jms 2). Two great teachings that came from the Reformation recovery of justification were these: (1) belief that one could have confidence that one was certainly justified ("assurance of salvation") and (2) belief that the justified sinner could never become unjustified ("security of the believer"). During the medieval period, both these were vigorously denied, and they continue to be matters disputed by Christians of today.

REFLECTION: Why focus on justification as the legal concept of the "declaration of righteousness"? Why distinguish between "justification by faith" and "justification by grace"?

PRAYER: *God, You justify all those who come to You by faith in Jesus Christ's death on their behalf. Thank You for the gift of righteousness and forgiveness through Our Lord. Amen.*

38. Adoption

He predestined us to be adopted through Jesus Christ for Himself, according to His favor and will, to the praise of His glorious grace that He favored us with in the Beloved.   Ephesians 1:5-6

DEFINITION: Adoption means that God grants family status and benefits, such as access to the Father and a spiritual inheritance, to all who are justified. The emphasis is on a personal relationship with God as Father brought about through the Holy Spirit.

In the Hebrew Scriptures the children of Israel were collectively called God's "son" (Ex 4:22-23; Hs 11:1). The modern custom of a childless couple taking a biologically unrelated infant and legally making it their own was unknown in biblical times. Yet in the first-century world, a wealthy but childless Roman man might adopt a young adult male of good standing in order to maintain the family name and estate. This differs markedly from the New Testament concept. First, the heavenly Father already has a Son (by nature); second, believers as adopted sons and daughters had nothing good in them to commend them to the Father. Our adoption into the family of God is a mark of His love (by grace).

Paul is the only New Testament writer explicitly to use the vocabulary of adoption. The Greek word literally means "placement as a son." The five instances in which this occurs are as follows:

- Rm 8:15—emphasizing the Spirit's role and the difference between slavery and adoption.
- Rm 8:23—emphasizing God's future gift to His adopted children: the resurrection body.
- Rm 9:4—emphasizing the nation Israel's role as God's adopted son.

- Gl 4:5-6—emphasizing the right of God's adopted children to call Him *Abba* (Daddy).
- Eph 1:5-6—emphasizing God's sovereign grace in choosing those whom He would adopt.

There is a close relationship between regeneration and adoption. The first focuses on the new moral nature and spiritual life received by believers; the latter centers on the close relationship with God that believers now enjoy as His "adopted kids."

Other New Testament teachings imply adoption without using the term. Above all is Jesus' teaching in the Sermon on the Mount. His disciples are to call on God as their Father, as in the Lord's Prayer (Mt 6:5-13). Further, they are to imitate their Father's character (Mt 5:9,44-48) and to trust in His loving provision for them (Mt 6:25-34). Jesus' most beloved story, usually called "The Prodigal Son," vividly portrays the heavenly Father's love to those who do not deserve Him (Lk 15:11-31).

On a more somber note, the author of Hebrews reminded his readers that all God's adopted children are to expect His discipline: "If you are without discipline—which all receive—then you are illegitimate children and not sons.... But He does it for our benefit, so that we can share His holiness" (Hb 12:8,10). Because the heavenly Father will succeed in His wonderful plan for His adopted children ("bringing many sons to glory"), His unique Son Jesus "is not ashamed to call them brothers" (Hb 2:10,11).

REFLECTION: Adoption is the greatest privilege the gospel brings. Do you agree with this claim? Why or why not? How often do you think of yourself as Jesus' adopted brother or sister?

PRAYER: *Heavenly Father, I call on You as my Father because You have welcomed me as your beloved child. Therefore I am bold to come. Help me to see all believers as my brothers and sisters in God's family, one day gloriously united in our Father's home. Amen.*

39. Faith

For God loved the world in this way: He gave His One and Only Son, so that everyone who believes in Him will not perish but have eternal life.

John 3:16

DEFINITION: Gospel faith means trust, reliance, confidence, or commitment. Jesus Christ, specifically His death in saving sinners, is the object of such belief. This must be distinguished from "assent" (belief that facts are true). Loyalty and devotion are included in genuine faith.

In the Old Testament, forms of "faith" or "believe" occur rarely, fewer than 50 times in all. (A key example is Genesis 15:6, noting Abraham's commitment to God's word or promise.) A broader picture emerges in the New Testament. The verb "believe" (Greek *pisteuo*) and the noun "faith" (Greek *pistis*) each occur more than 200 times. Usage among biblical writers varies. For example, the Gospel of John never uses the noun "faith," always the verb "believe."

"Faith" has a variety of possible meanings. Thus "the faith" (1 Tm 3:9) can be used as a shortcut to refer to "the Christian religion as a system of beliefs". Also *pistis* may refer to the quality of "faithfulness" in God or in human beings (Rm 3:3; Gl 5:22). All these are clearly superior to faith as mere assent to truth, which even demons have (Jms 2:19).

For the most part, however, "to believe" or "to have faith" means to place complete confidence in Jesus Christ. This focuses on individual commitment to Him as a person (Lord, Son of God, Savior). It also includes trusting in His death and resurrection as God's provision for one's own sins. Of special importance is the combination "believe" plus the Greek preposition meaning "into." This is usually translated "believe in," but the phrase, literally "believe into," shows the object into which confidence is placed. John's Gospel makes much of this:

To trust in Jesus' name: John 1:12; 2:11	To trust in Jesus: John 2:11 (Gl 2:16)
To trust in God's Son: John 3:16,36 (1 Jn 5:10)	To trust in the Son of Man: John 9:35
To trust in Me [Jesus]: John 6:35; 7:38; 11:25	To trust in God: John 14:1

Such faith is never considered a meritorious work; rather, it is the instrument or condition for God's work. Further, faith or believing in Scripture always has a specific object. Jesus is the One in whom faith is placed (New Testament emphasis) or else God's personal word or promise is believed (Old Testament emphasis). Such faith is highlighted in the great faith chapter of the New Testament, Hebrews 11, which recounts the heroes of faith who accomplished much. ("By faith," a single word in the original, occurs some 18 times in this chapter, and always as the first word of a new sentence.)

Where does faith come from? Is everyone naturally capable of faith, or is saving faith itself a gift from God? Many earnest followers of Christ have echoed the cry of a distraught father to Jesus: "I do believe! Help my unbelief" (Mk 9:24). Paul clearly believed that saving faith comes only in response to someone hearing God's word proclaimed; therefore none will be saved merely by the light of nature or the light of conscience. "So faith comes from what is heard, and what is heard comes through the message about Christ" (Rm 10:17; see Eph 2:8-9).

REFLECTION: Do you distinguish between "saving faith" as discussed in this study, and "temporal faith" (believing that God will care for a time-bound situation)? When did you first truly believe?

PRAYER: Lord Jesus, Grant me that faith in You alone that is the instrument by which salvation and a relationship with God—Father, Son, and Spirit—are eternally kept. In Your name, amen.

VII.CHURCH (and DISCIPLESHIP)

The American ideal has often portrayed the solitary individual succeeding against all odds by diligent effort. As heirs of the Reformation, evangelical Christians have championed the truth that each person is individually responsible for his or her own salvation. An unfortunate consequence of these twin forces is that "Sunday church" has often become merely an aggregate of individuals. They view church as simply a means to an end, no more connected to each other than passengers on an airplane flight. They think of themselves as "Lone Ranger" Christians.

The picture emerging from the New Testament is radically different. The local church is an expression of the body of Christ, with individual members contributing to the good of the family of faith and sharing in—and drawing life from—the whole. Family language flows from virtually every page of the Epistles. Evidently the first generation of Christians understood that the Christian life could not be lived in isolation. There was no such thing as a Christ follower who was not actively involved in the life of a congregation of believers.

At the beginning of the twenty-first century, many encouraging signs are emerging that "life together" is gaining new appreciation. Many believers are expressing longing for authenticity and community with each other. They are discovering that Christian discipleship works only in the context of church, a truth as old as the Book of Acts. This is reflected in the six following studies of this section.

40. Baptism

In Him you were also circumcised with a circumcision not done with hands, by putting off the body of flesh.... Having been buried with Him in baptism, you were also raised with Him through faith in the working of God, who raised Him from the dead.

Colossians 2:11-12

DEFINITION: Baptism is the initiation ceremony into Christianity in which one is marked publicly by water in the name of the Father, Son, and Spirit, symbolizing new life in Christ as well as pictorially re-presenting Christ's own death, burial, and resurrection.

Many of the world's religions as well as important social organizations include an initiation ceremony. This serves the important function of separating those who are "in" from those who are "out." Such identity markers play a crucial role in the group's self-understanding. One of the great scandals in Christian history has been that the ritual Christ intended for all His followers to share has become the subject of division and bitterness, as noted below.

At least the following facts of consensus about baptism have emerged:

- Baptism is a ritual performed with water because of Christ's command.
- Unlike the Jewish initiation ritual of circumcision, baptism is equally for females and males.
- The name of the Father, Son, and Spirit is called over the one baptized (Mt 28:19-20).
- True Christian baptism is to occur only once in a lifetime (see "one baptism" in Eph 4:5).
- Water baptism is *for* (= *identified with* or *because of*) the forgiveness of sins (Ac 2:38).

Much more difficult are other issues that have divided believers through the centuries.

1. *Who is eligible to be baptized?* Baptists in particular believe the only proper candidates are those who have already personally professed faith; others believe that for infants, the faith of the parents is sufficient (along the lines of Israelite parents presenting their sons for circumcision).

2. *Who is eligible to baptize?* Liturgical traditions have emphasized that baptism is a *church* ritual, and only those authorized by a local church (or denomination), usually ordained ministers, may perform baptism; others believe baptism is a *Christian* ritual that may be performed by any other Christian, spontaneously by request.

3. *What is the proper means of baptism?* Baptists, of course, note that immersion is the best way to portray death, burial, and resurrection (Rm 6:3-4); others emphasize that the Bible nowhere dictates the method and point to biblical images of sprinkling (Hb 10:22; 1 Pt 1:2).

4. *Does baptism have value as a sacrament?* Baptists and many others view baptism as simply an ordinance, an act of obedience ordained by Christ; many others see baptism as a "means of grace" by which Christ does something supernatural in the life of the person being baptized (strengthening and confirming faith); in general, evangelical believers have resisted the teaching that the act of baptism itself is necessary for salvation, that is, "baptismal regeneration."

Despite these challenges, it remains that Christians everywhere recognize water baptism as the mark that one has begun a life of following after Jesus. Further, the New Testament has no examples of unbaptized Christians. Although the topic is often confusing, thinking about one's baptism should be a cause of joy.

REFLECTION: What, if anything, have you decided about these four areas of disagreement? Is there someone with whom you should discuss these matters? When did you receive Christian baptism?

PRAYER: *Lord Jesus, thank You for commanding baptism as a way to mark the beginning of a life of following You. Help me to be true to my baptismal confession. In Your name I pray. Amen.*

41. Lord's Supper

And He took bread, gave thanks, broke it, gave it to them, and said, "This is My body, which is given for you. Do this in remembrance of Me." In the same way He also took the cup after supper and said, "This cup is the new covenant established by My blood; it is shed for you."   Luke 22:19-20

DEFINITION: The Lord's Supper, also called Holy Communion or the Eucharist, is the fellowship ritual in which assembled Christians eat bread and drink from the fruit of the vine in worship, showing their participation in Christ's death and life, as well as their life with one another.

Jesus asked His disciples to eat the bread and to drink the cup in memory of Him and His death. He taught that His death implemented the New Covenant prophesied in Jeremiah 31:31-33. Each biblical covenant had its God-ordained sign, and the sign of the New Covenant is the Lord's Supper. Baptism and the Lord's Supper are the only two ordinances (or sacraments) because they are the only rituals explicitly commanded by Jesus. Sadly, the ceremony meant to symbolize the unity of believers has become a matter of debate and contention.

At least the following facts of common consent emerge:

- The Lord's Supper is a ritual performed with bread and the cup by Christ's command.
- Something recognizable as bread and wine (fermented or not) is to be eaten and drunk.
- Unlike the annual Jewish Passover, Communion is to be observed "often" (1 Co 11:26).
- The Lord's Supper remembers both the Lord's death and His second coming (1 Co 11:26).
- The Supper is to be observed reverently and with self-examination (1 Co 11:28).

Devout students have arrived at divergent understandings in other aspects of the Supper.

1. *Who is eligible to partake of the Supper?* Some highly restrict it to the baptized members of the particular congregation celebrating together; others believe it should be open for every baptized person present; yet others welcome all, even those not yet openly Christian.

2. *Who is eligible to lead the Supper?* Traditionally, only ordained ministers—those authorized by a church or denomination—have led the Supper; others see no such restriction in Scripture.

3. *What setting is appropriate for the Supper?* Many have emphasized that this is a *church* ordinance and therefore limit the observance to recognized church services; others see it as a *Christian* celebration that can be enjoyed, for example, in retreat settings or in home groups.

4. *How often should the Supper be observed?* The first Christians probably celebrated weekly (Ac 2:46; 20:7), and many follow this pattern today; others observe the Supper once a month or several times a year; a few limit it to an annual observance.

5. *Does Communion have value as a sacrament?* Many view it as simply an ordinance, an act of worship ordained by Christ; others see it as a "means of grace" by which Christ supernaturally works in the lives of those partaking by strengthening and confirming their faith. Evangelical believers have resisted the teaching that eating the Supper is a way to receive Christ or that the bread and cup of Communion are transformed into the essence of Christ's body and blood.

Despite these challenges, throughout the ages thoughtful Christians have recognized celebrating Holy Communion to be the central act of worship in which they participate.

REFLECTION: What, if anything, have you decided about these five areas of disagreement? Is there someone with whom you should discuss these matters? How important is Communion for you?

PRAYER: *Lord Jesus, thank You for commanding the Lord's Supper as an act of worship, remembering Your death so that I might live in fellowship with You and other believers. Amen.*

42. Evangelism and Missions

Sing to the LORD, praise His name; proclaim His salvation from day to day. Declare His glory among the nations, His wonderful works among all peoples.   Psalm 96:2-3

DEFINITION: The "Great Commission" of Christ's church in the world is for local churches and individuals to proclaim the good news that Jesus is Lord and Savior, making disciples and establishing congregations, and expressing love to neighbors through works of compassion.

Jesus said, "As the Father has sent me, I also send you" (Jn 20:21). The English word "mission" is based on the Latin term for "send." The ongoing mission of witnessing—through word and deed—to Christ's lordship and urging others to become His followers is based on Jesus' "Great Commission." After His resurrection, Jesus expressed this command in a variety of ways. The two best-known texts are in Matthew and in Acts. In Matthew 28:19-20, He focused on the need to "make disciples" and the promise of His presence. In Acts 1:8, He centered on the call to "be My witnesses" and the promise of the Spirit's power to accomplish the task. Both passages envision the spread of churches throughout the entire world.

Evangelism in English is related to the Greek word *euangelion*, ordinarily translated "gospel" or "good news." (See the article on gospel.) Evangelism therefore necessarily means sharing the good news about Jesus' death for sinners and His resurrection as the living Lord (that is, witnessing to one's own encounter with Christ). If it is to be meaningful, evangelism must also include a call to believe the gospel and begin a life of Christian discipleship. This twofold message is often noted as proclamation and invitation. Evangelism, of course, is the responsibility of local churches as well as of individual believers. Paul reminded Timothy to "do the work of an evangelist" (2 Tm 4:5).

Christ's command to love one's neighbor as oneself (the second of the Great Commandments, Mt 22:39) is included in the church's mission. Jesus healed the sick and fed the hungry, and following Him includes continuing such ministries. Wherever churches have gone, hospitals have been built, schools have opened, and the material needs of humans—often in cases of natural disaster—have been met. This is frequently called the "social gospel," and such good works help make the "preached gospel" believable. After all, the Christian message is about a Savior who transforms sinners into persons who love both God and their neighbors.

The social gospel without the preached gospel will not result in lives transformed by the Word of God. But the preached gospel without the social gospel mistakenly supposes that the church's only business is "saving souls." Thus, when Jesus taught about the time when He will judge between "sheep and goats," all the criteria He named were along the lines of the social gospel (Mt 25:31-46).

What is the difference between evangelism and missions? This is a matter of degree rather than kind. When a church or individual takes the gospel to people of another language or culture or nation, it may be called "missions." When the message is shared to those within one's own social group, it is called "evangelism."

REFLECTION: How is your local church involved in evangelism and missions? How comfortable are you in witnessing for Christ? With whom do you need to share the message of the gospel?

PRAYER: Lord, help me to take Your Great Commission seriously and personally. Would You give me today the opportunity to communicate the gospel to someone without Christ? Amen.

43. Sanctification

For I am the LORD your God, so you must consecrate yourselves and be holy because I am holy.   *Leviticus 11:44*

Pursue peace with everyone, and holiness—without it no one will see the Lord.   *Hebrews 12:14*

DEFINITION: Sanctification is the process or result of being made holy. Places, things, and persons set apart for God and His use are "sanctified." God's holiness includes moral perfection; thus, holy persons are becoming more Godlike or Christlike in virtue and affections.

For many Christians, sanctification is an outdated word that conjures up uptight old ladies shaking their heads in disapproval of everything joyful or fun. While the word "sanctification" may not be capable of rehabilitation in English, the meaning behind the term is utterly important for Christian disciples. Sanctification simply means becoming Christlike in character. And if someone is not becoming more Christlike, it is problematic whether he or she has truly believed.

In the epistles, a frequent designation for all believers is "saints" or "holy ones" or "sanctified ones" (Rm 1:7; Php 1:1). Sainthood is not limited to an upper tier of more pious believers; rather, all Christians are already set aside for God and are becoming more virtuous as they grow in godliness. Sanctification (spiritual growth) is the complement to regeneration (spiritual birth). At the new birth, God gives one a new heart that desires to know and love Him, longing for obedience to Him, and willingness for worship and prayer.

Sanctification is the work of the Holy Spirit in the life of regenerate persons enabling "both to will and to act for His good purpose" (Php 2:13). Consider the following "holy terms" vocabulary of the New Testament:

- The adjective *holy* (as in *Holy* Spirit) is the Greek *hagios* (Jn 14:26).
- The word *saints* is the Greek *hagioi* (Ac 9:32).
- The verb *sanctify* (or *make holy*) is the Greek *hagiazo* (Hb 10:10).
- The noun *sanctification* (or *holiness*) is the Greek *hagiosmos,* occurring 10 times (Rm 6:19,22; 1 Co 1:30; 1 Th 4:3,4,7; 2 Th 2:13; 1 Tm 2:15; Hb 12:14; 1 Pt 1:2).

Sincere believers have often disagreed about the normal process of sanctification. Those from "holiness" traditions as well as those with Pentecostal or Charismatic beliefs emphasize a second work of grace after regeneration or a baptism by the Spirit empowering believers both to be holy and to do great acts of ministry. Others note that regeneration (birth) necessarily implies that sanctification (growth) will follow, and see a Christian's life of discipleship as one of gradual maturing. The English Puritans famously described Christian growth as a constant interplay between "mortification" (saying no to temptations; "killing" one's sinful "flesh") and "vivification" (allowing the Holy Spirit's life-giving power to work in one's life). For these Christians in particular, the struggle against the flesh that Paul outlined in Romans 7:14-25 was a present reality, and sanctification would never be complete in this lifetime. Paul's ultimate confidence was unmistakable, however. "I am sure of this, that He who started a good work in you will carry it on to completion until the day of Christ Jesus" (Php 1:6).

REFLECTION: Would you be offended or pleased if someone called you holy? What if they called you Christlike? Is there a difference? What does it mean that you are already a saint?

PRAYER: Holy Spirit of God, without Your sanctifying presence and power, I will never grow in godliness. Give me Your grace this day to become more like Jesus. Amen.

44. Gifts of the Spirit

Based on the gift they have received, everyone should use it to serve others, as good managers of the varied grace of God. If anyone speaks, his speech should be like the oracles of God; if anyone serves, his service should be from the strength God provides.

1 Peter 4:10-11

DEFINITION: At the time of the new birth, the Holy Spirit gives one or more special abilities to the believer, enabling him or her to build up other believers in the context of the local congregation. All believers are responsible for discovering, developing, and using their spiritual gifts.

The greatest of all God's gifts is the Spirit Himself, the mark that we belong to God (Rm 8:9). Thanks to the spread of Pentecostal and Charismatic congregations, Christians have recently become more aware of the importance and place of the gifts of the Holy Spirit. The word translated "gift" is *charisma* in Greek. Thus, every Christian is in some sense charismatic because every believer has a spiritual gift.

The quotation from Peter above shows that the charismatic gifts are of two basic sorts: speaking and serving. All other instances of *charisma* in the New Testament are in Paul's letters. The most helpful discussion of gifts is in Romans 12:3-8. The following truths are evident:

- Every Christian already has at least one such gift of the Spirit.
- Gifts are not identical with natural talents, because gifts are supernaturally bestowed.
- Gifts are to be used to build up the body of Christ not to exalt the gifted individual.
- The gifts include prophecy, service, teaching, exhorting, giving, leading, and showing mercy.

Much more controversial is Paul's teaching in 1 Corinthians 12–14, concentrating on two spiritual gifts: speaking in tongues and prophecy. Pentecostal and Charismatic teachings have brought to the forefront several important questions.

1. *Is "speaking in tongues" the spiritual gift that normally shows one has been "baptized by the Spirit"?* Pentecostals answer yes, based on Acts 2. Others have answered no, based on 1 Corinthians 12, believing that "baptism by one Spirit" happens at conversion, not later, and that Paul did not regard tongues as for every believer (1 Co 12:13,30).

2. *Is "speaking in tongues" in Acts the same as in 1 Corinthians?* Pentecostals answer yes. Others have seen great differences. For example, in Acts no translation or interpretation was necessary, but for the Corinthians someone with the gift of interpretation was required when tongues were spoken in public worship (1 Co 14:27-28).

3. *Is "speaking in tongues" as currently experienced the same as in the first century?* Pentecostals and many others answer, "Yes, this is the Holy Spirit at work." Some say, "No, modern tongues are at best psychologically induced." (But see 1 Co 14:4,39, in which speaking in tongues at least privately was never to be forbidden.)

What should not be missed in thinking about spiritual gifts is that each believer is to seek to be empowered ("filled") with the Spirit on an ongoing basis, as Paul taught in Ephesians 5:18. Further, all believers should seek to discover and develop their spiritual gifts as well as their natural talents in order to serve other believers and to bring glory to God.

REFLECTION: How well do you understand your spiritual gift(s)? How do you build up other believers through using your gifts? What have you decided about the questions listed above?

PRAYER: *Holy Spirit of God, Your presence in my life is God's great gift to me. Help me use Your other gifts in ways that honor You and build up others in Christ's body. Amen.*

45. Fruit of the Spirit

But the fruit of the Spirit is love, joy, peace, patience, kindness, goodness, faith, gentleness, self-control. Against such things there is no law.   Galatians 5:22-23

DEFINITION: The fruit of the Spirit refers to the character traits growing in believers as they mature. The Spirit produces these. Further, these traits are all attributes of Jesus Christ that the Gospels report concerning Him; therefore the fruit of the Spirit is another term for Christlike character.

Both Testaments contain lists of virtues that God expects His people to exhibit (Mic. 6:8; 2 Pt 1:5-7). Often these refer to specific actions: obey God's words; pray; follow the Ten Commandments; tell others about Jesus. The fruit of the Spirit, however, is more about inner character, reflecting a heart being transformed into Christ's moral likeness. There is no essential difference between growth in sanctification and growth in the fruit of the Spirit.

Both the "gifts of the Spirit" and the "fruit of the Spirit" are empowered by the Spirit working in cooperation with the individual believer, yet they differ significantly as well. The Spirit's gifts are capable of misuse and abuse. The Corinthians, who lacked no spiritual gift, were at the same time divided and "people of the flesh" (1 Co 1:7; 3:1-4). In fact, Jesus warned that flashy gifts such as prophesying, exorcism, and miracle working might be counterfeited (Mt 7:21-23). The Devil, masquerading as an angel of light, is well able to perform supernatural deeds through willing human agents (2 Co 11:14; 2 Th 2:9-11).

The fruit of the Spirit, however, can't be faked. The Devil has neither the desire nor the power to transform people into Christ's moral likeness. Many Bible students have noted that the word "fruit" is singular and that the primary character quality God desires is love (***agape***, see the article on love). When love is exposed to the various demands of life, it expresses itself as joy, peace, patience, and so on. A useful illustration from everyday physics may be helpful. Pure light is composed of all the colors of the rainbow. These colors are not seen, however, until a prism breaks white light into its components. So it is with the believer. The Spirit's fruit enables us to grow in loving God and our neighbors, and such love will be expressed in the manner most appropriate to the situation.

REFLECTION: Which aspect of the Spirit's fruit do you personally need the most for today? Evaluate your life over the past month. Which aspect of the fruit is the Spirit developing in you?

PRAYER: *Holy Spirit, I know that You long for me to be one in whom spiritual fruit is growing. Help me live today aware that You are empowering me to grow in Christ's likeness. Amen.*

Fruit of the Spirit

Love

Joy
Peace
Patience
Kindness
Goodness
Faith
Gentleness
Self-control

Daily Experiences

VIII. LAST THINGS

Teaching on the fulfillment of Bible prophecy still brings a crowd. Sometimes the approach is sensational. Well-meaning Christians (who understand that they shouldn't read horoscopes or go to fortune tellers) sometimes fall prey to preachers with the latest twist on the signs of the times. This becomes their way to peer into the crystal ball of the future. It is a matter of both amusement and consternation that thousands of sincere Christians have formulated opinions about last things based on popular novels rather than by study of Scripture. Date setters have abounded through 2,000 years of Christian history. So far, all of them have been terribly wrong. Christ's cause has often suffered great embarrassment from overzealous prophets.

Study of Christ's coming often generates more heat than light. Yet Christians of many different views about the details share common ground. The Apostles' Creed rightly included the words, "He shall come to judge the living and the dead." The seven articles that follow are meant to emphasize the common ground that Christians throughout the ages have found in Scripture. Inevitably, some of the areas of controversy have been touched on.

Whatever your perspective on the tribulation (pre-trib, post-trib, or other) and on the millennium (amill, premill, or other), you should recall that equally devout, Bible-believing Christians have taken an opposite view—and that opposing views can't both be right. Perhaps we should all agree to be "pan-trib" and "pro-mill," that is, the tribulation will "pan out" according to God's plan, not ours, and we can all be for ("pro") the millennium, even if we disagree about whether it is literal or spiritual. Our responsibility is to live now with the awareness that earthly life is preparation for eternity.

46. Glorification

So it is with the resurrection of the dead: Sown in corruption, raised in incorruption; sown in dishonor, raised in glory; sown in weakness, raised in power; sown a natural body, raised a spiritual body.

1 Corinthians 15:42-44

DEFINITION: Glorification involves two balanced but distinct aspects. First is God's work of transforming believers at death so that all sin is removed and they are fit to be in His presence; second is His gift of the resurrection body, received by saints only at Christ's return.

"Glorification" may be as old-fashioned sounding as "sanctification," but it is just as important for today's believers to understand. *Glorification* is the necessary complement to *justification*, just as *sanctification* completes *regeneration*. New spiritual life (regeneration) is completed by spiritual growth (sanctification). And justification (God's declaration of legal righteousness) is completed by glorification (God's transformation into perfect righteousness). Paul made this point by affirming, "Those He justified, He also glorified" (Rm 8:30).

The noun "glorification" does not actually appear in the New Testament. The noun "glory" (*doxa*) and the verb "glorify" (*doxazo*) are frequent. In most instances, they refer to God's glory and emphasize that human beings have as our purpose glorifying or praising God. (See the article on glory.) Yet glorification is appropriate as a summary word to describe God's future work in the believer, when He completes in heaven everything that He has begun in our lives on earth.

The Scriptures only hint at what it will mean for sin to be finally removed:

- "Blessed are the pure in heart, because they will see God" (Mt 5:8).

- "Now we see indistinctly, as in a mirror, but then face to face" (1 Co 13:12).
- "Blessed are the dead who die in the Lord from now on.... Let them rest from their labors, for their works follow them!" (Rv 14:13).

The longest passage dealing with the *intermediate* state of glorification (the period after a believer dies but before Christ's return) is 2 Corinthians 5:1-10. There Paul implies that believers will appear before the judgment seat of Christ after their death (v. 10; see also 1 Co 3:12-15).

Jesus was the first (and thus far only) human to be raised and given a glorified body that can no longer die. At His return, He will raise the saints and give them resurrection bodies like His. The longest passage on the resurrection body is 1 Corinthians 15:12-58. Paul maintained that there is continuity between our earthly body and our resurrection ("spiritual") body, just as there was continuity between Jesus' earthly body and His resurrection body. The continuity is like the connection between a seed planted in the earth and the plant that grows out of the seed (1 Co 15:34-44). The main point is that "we will also bear the image of the heavenly man [Jesus]" (1 Co 15:49).

The Christian doctrine of glorification is well summarized in Philippians 3:21: "He will transform the body of our humble condition into the likeness of His glorious body, by the power that enables Him to subject everything to Himself."

REFLECTION: Why is it important to keep in mind that glorification includes two aspects: moral-spiritual as well as bodily transformation. How much do you look forward to being glorified?

PRAYER: Lord Jesus, I long for the day when I will see You face-to-face because all trace of sin will be gone from my life. Praise You for the glorious promise of the resurrection. Amen.

47. Rapture

For the Lord Himself will descend from heaven with a shout, with the archangel's voice, and with the trumpet of God, and the dead in Christ will rise first. Then we who are still alive will be caught up together with them in the clouds to meet the Lord in the air.

1 Thessalonians 4:16-17

DEFINITION: The rapture refers to the teaching that believers living at Christ's return will not miss the resurrection, but will be caught up alive to meet the Lord in the air, transformed into a resurrection state without going through the experience of bodily death.

The word "rapture," like "Trinity," cannot be found in the Bible. Yet like Trinity, it expresses a perfectly wonderful biblical teaching. Rapture is based on the Latin translation of the verb translated "caught up" in English. Paul's teaching on the rapture was his reply to the distress of new converts: Had believers who died before Christ's return missed the blessings associated with that wonderful event? His answer was that, far from missing out, the dead would rise first, preceding all others, and only then will believers still living rise to meet the Lord.

All who take the Bible seriously believe in the rapture. What has become a matter of debate and contention is whether Paul was talking about an event more or less simultaneous with Christ's glorious return or whether the rapture is an event preceding His coming by a period of several months or years (7 years or 3½ years have been often suggested; Rv 12:14; 13:5).

This latter interpretation, first proposed in the 1800s, is connected with a relatively recent interpretation of Scripture called "dispensationalism." According to this view, living Christians will be raptured to heaven before the most horrible part of the end times (associated with the antichrist). After the rapture, God will allow great tribulation to come on Jewish people, but the end result will be a massive turning to Christ by Jews. Then Jesus will return to earth accompanied by previously raptured Christians. In other words, the rapture is a private return of Christ for Christians, while His coming is a public return with Christians. This view sharply separates God's end-time plan for Gentile saints ("the church") and for Jewish people ("Israel").

The other, more long-standing, view notes that no single passage in Scripture clearly separates the "rapture" from the "second coming." In this view, although God has promised that believers (Jew and Gentile) will never experience His wrath, they have not been promised escape from tribulation instigated by the Devil and by evil men. After all, Jesus promised, "You will have suffering [tribulation] in this world" (Jn 16:33). Further, the traditional view affirms that the church—not Israel—is the culmination of God's end-time plan (Eph 2:21). Finally, the language of 1 Thessalonians 4:16 ("shout" and "trumpet of God") suggests actions that in other passages are related to Christ's public second coming (1 Co 15:51-52). The following diagram shows the two major competing timelines proposed for understanding the rapture and the second coming.

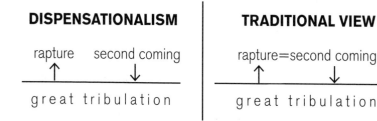

DISPENSATIONALISM	TRADITIONAL VIEW
rapture second coming	rapture=second coming
↑ ↓	↑ ↓
great tribulation	great tribulation

REFLECTION: What is the main point that Paul made in the "rapture passage"? How do you react to Christians who have a different view of the timeline of the rapture than you do?

PRAYER: *Lord Jesus, You alone know whether I will still be alive when the saints will be caught up to meet You in the air. Help me to live today as if this could be that very day. Amen.*

48. Tribulation and Wrath

For at that time there will be great tribulation, the kind that hasn't taken place from the beginning of the world until now and never will again! Unless those days were limited, no one would survive. But those days will be limited because of the elect. Matthew 24:21-22

DEFINITION: "Tribulation" refers to affliction (hardship or suffering) brought against God's people, either by life's circumstances or by evil forces, with "great tribulation" referring to end times troubles. "Wrath" refers to God's righteous anger against sin and evil.

In the New Testament, the word usually translated "tribulation" (Greek *thlipsis*) occurs more than 40 times, scattered throughout the Gospels, Acts, Epistles, and Revelation. It refers to the pressure or difficulty God's people ordinarily expect throughout life's journey. A sampling of such texts follows, with the Holman CSB translation for *thlipsis* placed in italics:

- "Then they will hand you over for *persecution,* and they will kill you" (Mt 24:9).
- "It is necessary to pass through many *troubles* on our way into the kingdom" (Ac 14:22).
- "Our momentary light *affliction* is producing for us ... glory" (2 Co 4:17).
- "I know your *tribulation* and poverty, yet you are rich" (Rv 2:9).

The New Testament writers recognized tribulation as a God-ordained process, expressed classically in Romans 5:3-5. There, *thlipsis* is the necessary foundation for producing endurance (and other virtues) and should therefore be an occasion of rejoicing, not despair.

What about the "great tribulation," the horrible end-time troubles? Actually, the phrase occurs in the Bible only four times, and two of these refer to past suffering by historical individuals (Ac 7:11; Rv 2:22). The others—which seem to be end-time references—are Matthew 24:21, quoted above, and Revelation 7:14. There, believers in Jesus (those who have "washed their robes and made them white in the blood of the Lamb") are seen "coming out of the great tribulation." In context, these persons did not escape the tribulation. The only divine guarantee of escape from the worldwide "hour of testing" is what Christ promised specifically only to first-century saints in Philadelphia (Rv 3:10). Yet many biblical scholars affirm, often on theological grounds rather than direct textual teaching, that believers will be removed from the end-time tribulation by the rapture. (See the article on the rapture.) Paul, for example, wrote, "God did not appoint us to wrath, but to obtain salvation through our Lord Jesus Christ" (1 Th 5:9).

This leads, then, to a consideration of "wrath" (Greek *orge*), occurring more than 30 times in the New Testament. Consider the following examples.

- "Brood of vipers! Who warned you to flee from the coming wrath?" (Mt 3:7).
- "We will be saved through Him from wrath" (Rm 5:9).
- "Jesus, who rescues us from the coming wrath" (1 Th 1:10).
- "If anyone worships the beast … he will also drink the wine of God's wrath" (Rv 14:9-10).

Clearly Jesus promised believers deliverance from God's wrath (just as the Israelites did not experience the 10 plagues on Egypt). Yet there seem to be no guarantees that Christians will escape tribulation (just as the Israelites endured the hostility of Pharaoh and the Egyptians).

REFLECTION: Do you think that Christians should escape tribulation in general? Why or why not? What about "the great tribulation"? Why do Christians expect to escape from God's wrath?

PRAYER: Lord Jesus, give me the grace to receive tribulation as a blessing, not a curse. Help me to grow from my troubles. Thank You that I will never experience Your wrath. Amen.

49.Second Coming

They said, "Men of Galilee, why do you stand looking up into heaven? This Jesus, who has been taken from you into heaven, will come in the same way that you have seen Him going into heaven."

Acts 1:11

DEFINITION: The second coming refers to the personal, visible, bodily, victorious return of Jesus Christ to earth as King of kings and Lord of lords.

The New Testament constantly teaches the second coming of Jesus Christ. The Greek term most often used is *parousia* (occurring more than 20 times in the New Testament). Jesus Himself used this term in Matthew 24:27,37,39. In the first century *parousia* referred to a king's royal visit. Less frequent are the terms *apokalupsis* ("revelation," as in 1 Co 1:7; 2 Th 1:7) and *epiphaneia* ("appearing," as in 1 Tm 6:14; Ti 2:13). The English terms "Parousia," "Apocalypse," and "Epiphany"—often used in the context of sermons on Bible prophecy—are obviously derived from the Greek terms.

His return will be *personal*. The very same Jesus who ascended into heaven will return (Ac 1:11). The closing words of Revelation point to this truth as well: "He who testifies about these things says, 'Yes, I am coming quickly.' Amen! Come, Lord Jesus! The grace of the Lord Jesus be with all the saints. Amen" (Rv 22:20-21). Any teaching that denies continuity between the Jesus who lived in history and the returning Christ is distorting the plain message of the New Testament.

His return will be *visible*. Some well-meaning interpreters have suggested that the events surrounding the destruction of Jerusalem and the temple in AD 70 fulfilled the prophecies of the second coming. Our Lord was clearly concerned about these events, for His Olivet Discourse (Mt 24–25) is full of specific prophecies about the fall of

Jerusalem. This was a divine judgment—tribulation and wrath—but they do not fulfill the promise that "every eye will see Him" (Rv 1:7).

His return will be *bodily.* Some interpreters have supposed that the descent of the Holy Spirit on the day of Pentecost (Ac 2) fulfills the promise of His second coming. But this would surely mean that all the apostles were wrong, because they thought Jesus' return was still in the future (Jms 5:7-8). Apparently this kind of teaching was prevalent in the first century, for Peter went to great lengths to counteract those scoffers who denied the coming of Jesus (2 Pt 3:3-9).

His return will be *victorious.* He will defeat all His enemies (Rv 19:11-21). He will raise even the wicked dead so that they will be judged (Jn 5:28-29). He will bestow on His people their final glory (Rm 8:18-19; Col 3:4).

Those who are not ready for the second coming will face catastrophe (Mt 24:36-51), yet no one can know that time until it arrives. In the Epistles, teaching on the second coming was meant to spur Christian people to lives of active service (1 Co 15:58). "We wait for the blessed hope and the appearing of the glory of our great God and Savior, Jesus Christ" (Ti 2:13).

REFLECTION: Does the thought of living until Christ's coming excite or alarm you? What actions should you take to get ready spiritually for His return?

PRAYER: *Exalted Lord, I confess to You that I believe You will return in power and glory. I believe You will come back to earth personally, visibly, bodily, and victoriously. Give me grace to live waiting for the blessed hope of Your second coming. In Your powerful name, Amen.*

50. Millennium

Blessed and holy is the one who shares in the first resurrection! The second death has no power over these, but they will be priests of God and the Messiah, and they will reign with Him for 1,000 years.

Revelation 20:6

DEFINITION: The millennium (Latin for 1,000 years) refers to the reign of God's people–especially martyrs–either spiritually before Christ's second coming or else literally after His return but before the last judgment and the new creation.

Revelation 20 is the only passage in the Bible that speaks about a 1,000-year period of saints ruling, yet this has been a matter of such great dispute that entire theological systems have been constructed based on particular interpretations of this chapter. Like "rapture," "millennium" is not found in the Bible, but it is a good term for referring to the 1,000 years of Revelation 20. Also, as with the rapture, everyone who takes the Bible seriously believes that there is such a thing as the millennium. Further, everyone understands that this millennium experience is greatly to be desired and that Christian martyrs are special beneficiaries of the millennium. The point of dispute is whether the text is meant to describe something literal that will occur on earth after Jesus' second coming or whether it is already occurring spiritually now.

Literal millennium. The earliest Christian scholars (second and third centuries AD) believed that when Christ returned victoriously, He would overthrow Rome (the harlot city Babylon of Revelation 17). He would rule over all the earth from the bride city, New Jerusalem, along with the resurrected Christian martyrs who had died opposing Rome. The usual name for this view is "historical premillennialism." This approach declined in the medieval period. It did not seriously come to prominence again until the 1800s with the rise of dispensationalism. (See the article on the rapture.) In its current form, the emphasis is usually on Jesus' rule over the earth from a literal but renovated Jerusalem, with converted people from Israel at the forefront, fulfilling Scriptural prophecies about a glorious future for national Israel (Isaiah 60—66; Ezekiel 40—48). This recent form is called "dispensational premillennialism."

Spiritual millennium. After the Roman emperors became supporters of Christianity rather than persecutors, it was no longer viable for Christians to interpret "harlot Babylon" as Rome. The great Bible scholar Augustine (early 400s) wrote his masterwork, *The City of God,* around the concept that the two cities "Babylon" and "New Jerusalem" have been in existence spiritually since the fall of mankind. Human history is the ongoing conflict between the two cities. Because of Christ's first coming, Satan has been largely defeated and Christian believers are now already enjoying the first taste of victory (Col 2:15). We are already "seated ... with Him in the heavens" spiritually (Eph 2:6). The common name for this view is "amillennialism." Many from Augustine's time until today have vigorously maintained it. A variation of this view is "postmillennialism," which emphasizes that the Christian missionary endeavor will be so successful that the world's peoples will generally turn to Christ before His second coming.

REFLECTION: What was the main point that John made in the "millennium passage"? How much difference should one's view of the millennium make in the way life is to be lived now?

PRAYER: Lord Jesus, Your word promises blessing on those who share in the first resurrection. I long for the full experience of reigning with You not just for 1,000 years but forever. Amen.

51.Final Judgment

Let them say among the nations, "The LORD is King!" Let the sea and everything in it resound; let the fields and all that is in them exult. Then the trees of the forest will shout for joy before the LORD, for He is coming to judge the earth.   *1 Chronicles 16:31-33*

DEFINITION: God through Christ will bring about the final verdict on all human beings, resulting in one of two eternal destinies: eternal joy in the presence of God (heaven) or eternal misery cast away from all hope of God and good (hell).

God's right to judge the whole world was firmly attested in the Old Testament. Worshipers of heathen gods thought of them as territorial and in control of only limited persons and places. But the Lord God of Israel, Maker of heaven and earth, was different. He created all persons and places; therefore all were accountable to Him. God's judgment is well developed in the Psalms (7:8; 96:10,13; 98:9). Ezekiel promised that God would judge Israel like a shepherd separating sheep and goats (Ezk 34:27-24). When Jesus lived on earth, He taught that the Father had entrusted to Him the responsibility of final judgment. "He [the Father] has granted Him [the Son] the right to pass judgment, because He is the Son of Man" (Jn 5:27). "When the Son of Man comes in His glory, and all the angels with Him, then He will sit on the throne of His glory. All the nations will be gathered before Him, and He will separate them one from another, just as a shepherd separates the sheep from the goats" (Mt 25:31-32).

When Christ comes again, all persons of all times will be raised and be judged by Him as King and Judge. He "will repay each one according to his works: eternal life" to some but "wrath and indignation" to others (Rm 2:6-8). Those who have been regenerated will receive eternal life with God, and will have shown it by their righteous works (Mt 16:27; Rv 22:12).

Yet Paul described the good works of some believers as like "gold, silver, [or] costly stones" but that of others as "wood, hay, or straw" (1 Co 3:12). Their works will be burned up, but they "will be saved; yet it will be like an escape through fire" (1 Co 3:15).

Those who were never regenerated will be condemned. "The one who believes in the Son has eternal life, but the one who refuses to believe in the Son will not see life; instead, the wrath of God remains on him" (Jn 3:36). The severity of their sentence will depend on the extent to which they knew God's righteous requirements (Mt 11:20-24; Rm 2:12).

Some Bible scholars have distinguished between several biblical descriptions of judgment and think there are different kinds and times of final judgment:

- The judgment of the nations—Matthew 25:31-46
- The judgment seat of Christ (or God)—Romans 14:10-12; 2 Corinthians 5:10
- The great white throne judgment—Revelation 20:11-15

Others believe that these are simply different accounts of one final general judgment at the end of all earthly life as we know it. In either case, God's people are to understand that we too will be judged and should therefore live in preparation for standing before God.

REFLECTION: One of the Devil's greatest triumphs is to stop people from thinking about their coming judgment. How much do you agree with this claim? How intentional are you about living in light of your coming judgment by Christ? How are you preparing to meet the Judge?

PRAYER: Lord Jesus, I humbly submit to you as Lord and Judge. By faith in You, I know I will not be condemned. Help me to live in light of my coming judgment before Your throne. Amen.

52. Heaven

For I will create a new heaven and a new earth; the past events will not be remembered or come to mind.　　　　　*Isaiah 65:17*
But based on His promise, we wait for new heavens and a new earth, where righteousness will dwell.　　　　　*2 Peter 3:13*

DEFINITION: Heaven is the supernatural location of God's presence displayed far beyond the earth, where the holy angels worship Him. After the last judgment and the renewal of all things, God will manifest His presence among the redeemed in "the New Jerusalem."

"Heaven and earth" (or "the heavens and the earth") describe the entire universe that God created (Gn 1:1). Yet the heavens are divided into the visible heavens—where the birds fly and the clouds form and the sun and moon and stars appear—and the invisible heavens—God's supernatural dwelling place (Ps 80:14; Is 66:1; Mt 5:12) and the home of holy angelic beings (Mt 24:36). God's will is done perfectly in heaven (Mt 6:10). Surprisingly, the Old Testament says little if anything about the righteous going to heaven when they die.

In the New Testament, however, heaven is a place where the righteous may store treasures (Mt 6:20). Another term for heaven in this sense is "paradise" (Lk 23:43; 1 Co 12:4; Rv 2:7). The exalted Lord Jesus is presently there, having "sat down at the right hand of the Majesty on high" (Hb 1:3), and He will return to earth from heaven (1 Th 4:16). Believers already lay claim to citizenship in heaven (Php 3:20; see Lk 10:20; Hb 12:23). Although Christ followers rightly understand that we will go to heaven when we die (waiting for the resurrection), the New Testament says very little about this condition. Paul simply called it being "with Christ" and something that was "far better" than earthly life (Php 1:23).

After the final judgment, Christ will make all things new, because "the elements will burn and will be dissolved" and "the heavens will be on fire and be dissolved" (2 Pt 3:10,12). The lovely description of the final everlasting home of resurrected human beings is not of a heaven "up there" but of heaven come down to earth, the city called new Jerusalem (Rv 21–22). God created mankind to live on earth, and so mankind will live eternally in a place in some ways like the original home of humankind in Eden, with a flowing river and the tree of life (Rv 22:1-2). Nothing could be more glorious than this description, even though we cannot now comprehend it: "The throne of God and of the Lamb will be in the city, and His servants will serve Him. They will see His face, and His name will be on their foreheads" (Rv 22:3).

Yet this place will be better than Eden, for it will mean that "God's dwelling is with men, and He will live with them. They will be His people, and God Himself will be with them and be their God" (Rv 21:3). This beautifully and perfectly fulfills one of God's great promises both to Israel and to Christians:

- "I will walk among you and be your God, and you will be My people" (Lv 26:12).
- "I will dwell among them and walk among them, and I will be their God, and they will be My people" (2 Co 6:16).

REFLECTION: What do you most look forward to about heaven (when your body dies)? What do you most look forward to about heaven (after all things are made new)?

PRAYER: Lord of heaven, I long for the time when at last Your will shall be done on earth as it is in heaven. Thank You for the promise of heaven where You will be present with Your people forever and we shall see You face-to-face, forever with You in glory. In Christ's name, amen.

IX. POSTSCRIPT

In the introduction, I made the following claim:
I have written from a broadly evangelical perspective. My treatment is sensitive to areas where there are major differences of opinion, such as dispensational eschatology, Calvinism, Pentecostal issues, and the sacraments or ordinances. On the other hand, I affirm as a foundation the classic confessions of the churches (the Apostles' Creed and the Nicene Creed) and the five pillars of the Reformation (salvation as taught in Scripture alone, by Christ alone, by grace alone, through faith alone, to the glory of God alone). If you relate positively to these beliefs and want to gain a better understanding of essential Christian terms, this book is for you.

It is up to you to judge how well this has been accomplished. Yet one final word is in order concerning the five pillars of the Reformation. These should be summarized, for they have everything to do with the way one thinks about eternal matters.

- Scripture Alone (Sola Scriptura): **The Bible alone teaches everything necessary for a person's salvation.**
- Christ Alone (Solus Christus): Salvation is accomplished by the work of the historical Jesus alone, for His sinless life and substitutionary death are entirely sufficient for salvation.
- Grace Alone (Sola Gratia): In salvation we are rescued from God's wrath by His undeserved favor through the supernatural work of the Holy Spirit.
- Faith Alone (Sola Fidei): Faith alone is the instrument through which Christ's righteousness is counted to us as satisfying God's perfect justice, and such saving faith is not a good work.
- Glory to God Alone (Soli Deo Gloria): Because salvation is from God and has been accomplished by God, it is for His glory and we are to praise Him always.

Christians are to live all of life before Him under His authority and for His glory. I have based my entire hope for God and good and eternity on these. How about you?